Linn's

Franklin D. Roosevelt: the Stamp-Collecting President

Brian C. Baur

Published by *Linn's Stamp News*, the largest and most informative stamp newspaper in the world. *Linn's* is owned by Amos Press Inc., 911 Vandemark Road, Sidney, Ohio 45365. Amos Press also publishes *Scott Stamp Monthly* and the Scott line of catalogs. Cover design by Veronica Schreiber.

Contents

Introduction

I have always been fascinated by the Franklin Delano Roosevelt era. The years 1933 to 1945 are to me the most hectic, frightening, hopeless and at the same time the most paced, safe and hopeful 12 years in American history.

When I was a youngster in school and first learned about the FDR era and its relevance to the America in which I was growing up, I was enthralled with learning all I could about the man and the efforts he made to make America a better place in which to live.

When I learned that Roosevelt was a stamp collector, I was even more impressed. I had been collecting stamps for three years or so, and was surprised and pleased to discover that FDR had been a stamp collector all his life. I was impressed that during the most tumultuous and dangerous time in the history of America, the president of the United States relaxed and recharged his batteries by going through his many stamp albums, covers and collections. He is shown examining a stamp from his collection in Figure 1.

The more I read about FDR, and especially the little items I found concerning his stamp collecting, the more interested in stamp collecting I became. I read about the president's great knowledge of the world and its geography, which he ascribed to his stamps. Consequently, when confronted with a place I never heard of, I would often first turn to a Scott *Specialized Catalogue of United States Stamps*. There I could find the place I was looking for and see its history through its stamps.

I discovered over the years many biographies about FDR and his presidency, and read them all with interest. In some of them I discovered that FDR not only collected stamps but was responsible for designing a handful of U.S. stamps issued during his tenure. I also learned that he personally approved every U.S. stamp that was issued during his 12 years in the oval office.

But there was little specific information concerning FDR and stamps, whether it was the stamps issued by the United

Figure 1. FDR looked upon the time he spent with his stamps as one of complete relaxation and rest.

States during his tenure or the stamps in his collections.

This lack of information puzzled me, because Franklin Roosevelt did much to make stamp collecting a respectable hobby in the 1930s. Stamps also shaped his outlook on many things and helped him through the most difficult ordeals of his life. However, no single book discussed the importance of the postage stamp to FDR.

I needed to know more about FDR and how stamps impacted his life. This led me to the Franklin D. Roosevelt Library in Hyde Park, New York, where FDR was born and is now buried. Here I was able to delve into the president's papers, including many items related to his stamp collections and the stamps issued during his tenure of office.

A veritable treasure-trove of information resulted in many field trips to the Roosevelt library and ultimately in the release of my first book, *Franklin D. Roosevelt and the Stamps of the United States, 1933-1945*, published by *Linn's Stamp News* in 1993. The book details the history of all the stamps issued by the United States during that time, and relates details and anecdotes about FDR's hands-on participation in all aspects of those stamps.

Ironically, when I first started my research at the FDRL, I envisioned the book that I have completed here. But the information concerning the FDR-era stamps was so great that I found myself writing about them instead. I didn't realize until I actually began putting the book together that I had in fact not written the book I had started out to write.

After completion of *Franklin D. Roosevelt and the Stamps of the United States, 1933-1945*, I knew I must write this book.

My next discovery was the four H.R. Harmer auction catalogs for the sale of the Roosevelt collection in 1946. These catalogs showed in vivid detail and descriptions the types of stamps that FDR collected.

The Harmer catalogs did much more than that, however. They also showed what kind of stamp collector Franklin Delano Roosevelt was. The sheer volume of covers and stamps in his collection, many thousands of them packed in boxes, showed that he resisted discarding any stamp that found its way to him and, like most collectors, longed for more time to sort through these thousands of stamps and add them to his albums. The pages in his many stamp albums clearly show that he not only studied his stamps in great detail but wrote all pertinent information about each stamp on the album page, including details on postmarks, issue dates, stamp varieties, colors and descriptions, and data about the area, person or event commemorated on the stamp.

The auction catalogs showed that FDR found any stamp interesting. Badly centered and perforated stamps that would be considered seconds to most collectors found their way into FDR's albums where they may be mounted alongside a pristine copy to show different printing or perforation varieties. An example is the Polish album page in Figure 2, showing different varieties and cancels of four stamps of the same issue. Often a used stamp would have only a portion of the postmark stamped on it, and FDR reveled in being able

Figure 2. This album page of Polish stamps shows how the president saved all varieties of the same postage stamps, no matter how small the difference was from stamp to stamp.

to puzzle out the original cancel. He frequently drew a completed version of the postmark next to the stamp.

The prices realized for each sale showed that the people of the United States held Franklin Roosevelt in high esteem, and bid far and above catalog values and estimates on items so they could have a memento from the president's collection.

Needless to say, the H.R. Harmer auction catalogs were indispensable to me in writing this book.

As the author of these books on Franklin D. Roosevelt and stamps, I am solely responsible for any errors or discrepancies in them, and invite and encourage readers to call them to my attention. It is my sincere hope that these books give accurate and interesting accounts of our "philatelic president." I am sure that there are fellow stamp collectors who are as curious as I am to learn more about FDR and stamps. I am equally sure that there are many noncollectors who have an interest in how stamps helped shape Franklin Roosevelt's thinking and knowledge. I hope I've shed light on these aspects of FDR's life.

— Brian C. Baur
Fergus Falls, Minnesota

For the Record

I would like to express my thanks to the staff at the Franklin D. Roosevelt Library in Hyde Park, New York, for their help during my days of researching at their fine library. Without their help and expertise I would probably not have located much of the information that makes up this book.

Thanks to Keith Harmer at Harmer of New York for help with information concerning the auctioning of FDR's collections in 1945-46.

Thanks also to the staff of the Chicago Heights Public Library for their help in securing microfilm and books from far-off places.

Of course my thanks to my family and friends for their support while this book was in progress. You know who you are. Also thanks to my stamp dealer Duane Larson of Rosemoor Stamps in Homewood, Illinois, for all of his help, conversation and encouragement.

Thanks to the "All American Alien Boy" Ian Hunter, for services rendered.

A very special thanks must go to Bill Hannegan of St. Louis, Missouri, for his help, encouragement, friendship and support. Also to newfound philatelic friend Michael Harkins, of Columbus, Georgia.

I also owe an eternal debt of gratitude to my new hometown of Fergus Falls, Minnesota — a great place to live, a great place to write. Thanks to the Fergus Falls public library, to Bud and Addie Thompson, Allen Hanson and all other people of the town.

A special thank you to those who responded to the article in an August 1996 issue of *Linn's Stamp News* and took the time to send items from Franklin Roosevelt's collections to be used as illustrations for this book. Their help is greatly appreciated, and this book would not have been possible without their generosity. They include LeRoy Reed, Robert B. Smith, Joseph P. Connolly, Sherwin Podolsky, Stan Glasofer, Leon Fink, W. Curtis Livingston, Shirley Morgan, Bernard Goldberg, Richard Greenberg, Herb Cantor, Bennett Brooke, Henry B. Scheuer, Chuck Hemrick, Fred Buza, Thomas P. Myers, Philip R. McCarty, Marc Gonzales, Walter Tuchman, Joseph Scafetta Jr., James K. McCartney, Jack Harwood, Armand Singer, Robert E. Morin, Max Statman, Enrique Trigueros and Mike Vining.

Finally, a book should never be published without a word of gratitude to the editor. My heartfelt thanks therefore to Donna Houseman, my editor at *Linn's*. Without Donna's help and efforts on my behalf, my writings would still be in a box on my bookshelf.

CHAPTER 1

The Roosevelt Family in America

History tells us that the founding father of the Roosevelt family in America was Claes Martenzen van Rosenvelt, who arrived in the New World from Holland sometime in the 1640s. Translated into English, his name means Nicholas, son of Martin, of the Rose Fields. Tradition of the time had sons taking, in addition to their baptismal name, the name of their father and the name of the area in which they resided.

Claes and his wife, Jannetje, had six children in America. The last son, Nicholas, owned and operated a flour mill in New York City and was eventually elected an alderman in 1690. At this time the "van" was dropped from the family name, and the accepted Americanization of it became Roosevelt.

Nicholas had two sons, Johannes, or John, who begat the Oyster Bay, or Theodore Roosevelt branch of the family, and Jacobus, or James (1692-1776), who begat the Hyde Park, or Franklin Roosevelt branch.

Jacobus Roosevelt's fifth son, Isaac (1726-94), was a businessman and banker who supported the cause of American independence. He served in the New York Provincial Congress and was a leading supporter of ratification of the U.S. Constitution. He is referred to in the Roosevelt family as "Isaac the Patriot." A portrait of Isaac is shown in Figure 3.

Isaac Roosevelt's son, James (1760-1847), operated a sugar refinery, but preferred country life to business. In 1818 he purchased Mount Hope, an estate located on the Hudson River just above Poughkeepsie in New York State.

James Roosevelt's son, Isaac (1790-1863), studied medicine but did not practice, it is said, because he could not abide human suffering. Isaac lived at Mount Hope the year round, and at age 37 married Mary Rebecca Aspinwall, who bore him a son, James, the next year.

James Roosevelt (1828-1900) was a lawyer and businessman who, like his grandfather, preferred the life of a country squire. He married Rebecca Howland in 1853, and in 1854 she bore him a son

Figure 3. FDR's great-great-grandfather Isaac Roosevelt, who was known in the family as Isaac the Patriot. This portrait hangs in the Roosevelt home in Hyde Park, New York. (Photo courtesy Roosevelt Library)

whom they gave the interesting name James Roosevelt Roosevelt.

In 1867 the elder James purchased an estate in Hyde Park, New York, which he named Springwood. From here, James directed his business dealings while devoting his time to the local school board, several community charities and serving as town supervisor. The house as it looks today is shown in Figure 4.

Rebecca Roosevelt died in 1876. After a few years alone, the 56-year-old James courted and married 23-year-old Sara Delano in October 1880.

Sara Delano was descended from prominent New England blood. The first of her family in America was Philippe de la Noye, from whom descended a seafaring family of whalers, sailors and merchant seamen.

On January 30, 1882, after 24 hours of labor, during which she almost died from an overdose of chloroform, Sara presented James with a son. "At quarter to nine my Sallie had a splendid large baby boy," James wrote. "He weighs 10 lbs., without clothes."[1]

The new arrival seemed destined by tradition to be named Isaac Roosevelt, but Sara balked at tradition, telling James that the name Isaac wasn't distinguished enough for their new son. They finally agreed to name the new baby Warren after Sara's father. Prior to the christening, however, Sara was in contact with her older brother Warren Delano III, whose own son, Warren IV, died in early childhood at about the same time Sara's baby was expected. Warren III told his sister that he could not bear for her to call her new son Warren so soon after the death of his own son. After much discussion, Sara and James decided to name the new baby Franklin after Sara's uncle Franklin Delano.[2]

Figure 4. Springwood in Hyde Park, New York, has changed much since James Roosevelt purchased it in 1867. FDR's home as it looks today.

CHAPTER 2

The Genesis of a Stamp Collection

Sara Delano Roosevelt's father, Warren Delano II, was a seafarer, like most Delano men. While in his twenties, he entered into the China tea trade, piloting his own ship. By the time he was in his early thirties he had made a fortune from his China trade and purchased a large estate in Macau. He brought his bride, Catherine Lyman, whom he married in 1843 to live with him in Macau.

In 1851 the Delanos purchased Algonac, an estate near the Hudson River. Sara Delano was born at Algonac in 1854.

In 1857 a financial panic struck American business. Several banks and insurance companies failed. Although a wealthy man, Warren Delano found himself in the precarious position of looking at possible bankruptcy.

In 1859, at age 50, Delano left his wife and children to start over in the trade business. This time, however, the trade was opium, which was then touted for its medicinal value, especially during the American Civil War.

While in Hong Kong, Delano amassed a small collection of Hong Kong stamps for his daughter Sara. He sent her the stamps, hoping that they would take her mind off his absence until he made enough money to bring the family to him. Within two years, Delano was able to bring his family to Hong Kong. Sara spent 18 months reuniting with her father and adding to the stamp collection he had started, mounting the stamps in an album he had provided.

On her way back to New York, Sara traveled leisurely through Singapore, Paris and London. In each city, she acquired new stamps for her collection. Sara (circa 1869) is shown in Figure 5.

Within five years, Delano had amassed his second fortune and returned to Algonac to again retire to private life.

Delano's second fortune enabled Sara to travel around the world during her teen years. Her extensive travels gave her ample opportunity to add many foreign stamps to her collection. By the 1870s, however, other diversions began to take

Figure 5. Sara Delano, Franklin D. Roosevelt's mother, in 1867.

precedence for the young woman, now in her early twenties.

During this time, she gave the collection to her younger brother Frederic, who took to the hobby instantly and became a serious philatelist. Frederic is shown in Figure 6 in a photograph taken in 1930. He not only collected stamps but wrote up pertinent facts concerning the issuance of the stamp, the history of the people or events depicted, and the general history of the countries and areas he collected.

Besides the stamps of Hong Kong, Frederic added many rare Chinese stamps to the collection. He also added stamps to the collections of British and French stamps that Sara had begun, and started specialized collections of several South American countries.

Figure 6. Frederic Delano, who took over his sister Sara's collection of Hong Kong stamps and added to it.

Frederic was a keen philatelist. He collected stamps both on and off cover, and studied cancellations, postmarks and other postal markings, carefully writing up information on his collection.

Like Sara, Frederic Delano traveled extensively in Europe and other parts of the world. On these journeys, he added stamps to his collections, making inquiries concerning new issues and delving into the histories of older stamps. Trips to European countries presented the opportunity to track down elusive rarities and to fill in blank spaces in his albums. More importantly, they allowed him to gather information on the history of a stamp, its printing varieties, its usage and its postal markings.

Because stamps and stamp collecting were a mere 30 years old in 1870, it was quite possible for a rich young man like Frederic to build complete collections of many countries of the world. This is what he set out to do.

Under Frederic, the stamp collection begun by Warren Delano to keep his daughter busy while he was away in Hong Kong became both greatly enlarged and valuable. It continued to grow for some time.

CHAPTER 3

Young Franklin Roosevelt and Stamps

Franklin Roosevelt's birth into aristocracy in 1882 gave him many opportunities that other young men did not have. His education was put in the hands of a succession of Swiss and French governesses and tutors who, along with his mother's stories of her travels and adventures through China and the rest of the world, instilled in him a love for people and history.

By the time he was 9, he had made his first trip across the Atlantic to Germany, where his father annually spent six weeks at the spa Bad Nauheim.

No doubt due in part to the stories Sara told him about China and the stamps she accumulated as she toured the world, at age 9 young Franklin Roosevelt began his own stamp collection. He acquired stamps during his travels and he also enlisted the help of relatives who either lived in other countries or were traveling abroad.

One of the first examples of FDR's interest in stamps is a letter he wrote to Sara's older sister Dora and her husband Will Forbes who were traveling abroad in the spring of 1891:

"April 10, 1891
My Dear Aunt Doe . . . Please tell Uncle Will that if he has any foreign stamps that I should like to have them, as I have begun to make a collection."[1]

Young Franklin's curiosity about the countries that issued these stamps helped him in his collecting. Like his Uncle Frederic, he diligently logged the pertinent information about each stamp.

His penchant for learning about foreign places also led him to write to relatives and acquaintances to ask questions about the countries in which they lived. In a letter to a former governess who was living in Switzerland in 1893, Franklin asked who the president of Switzerland was and how the Federal Assembly and Senate operated.[2] He recorded the answers and added this information to his collection.

Uncle Frederic was impressed with the child's interest in stamps and the countries that issued them. Uncle Frederic was a good source of information for the young collector.

As a youth, Franklin Roosevelt collected many things, including birds nests and eggs. Later he collected the birds themselves, stuffing, mounting and keeping meticulous notes on their habits. He developed such a professional competency in ornithology that his collection became one of the most comprehensive ever made of the birds of the Hudson River Valley.

True to the Delano blood in him, FDR was also strongly attracted to the sea. He collected models and prints of whaling vessels, schooners, frigates and war ships.

His other collecting interests included lavishly produced miniature books from around the world, U.S. Navy paraphernalia and military insignias. He also maintained an affinity for sailing, dogs, horseback riding, reading and photography.

Frederic was so impressed with Franklin's interest in stamps that when his nephew turned 10 in 1892, he presented him with the stamp collections begun by Warren Delano for Sara.

Thus, at an early age, Roosevelt accumulated a collection of stamps that would be the envy of any philatelist of the time. He continued to add it, as attested to by a reminder of an April 2, 1892, order to the Scott Stamp and Coin Company of New York for $66.14. He had written the reminder in French in one of his school exercise books.[3]

During his youth, Roosevelt focused his attention on adding to the collection of Hong Kong stamps started by his mother and the specialized collections of China and countries of South and Central America given to him by Uncle Frederic. He began to branch off into other areas of South and Central America and to specialize in the stamps of Haiti and Santo Domingo.

In 1896, at the age of 14, Roosevelt left home to attend Groton School in Massachusetts. Already a year behind other boys his age because of Sara's reluctance to let go of her only child, he strove to become "one of the boys" at Groton. He tried to excel at sports and extracurricular activities, and deliberately got a few behavioral black marks on his record so he would fit in with the other boys. During this time, he added few stamps to his collections.

In the spring of 1898, with his close friend Lathrop Brown and another class member, FDR left school and enlisted in the U.S. Navy to fight in the Spanish-American War. The three youths had arranged for a pieman to smuggle them off the school grounds in his cart. When the day of escape came, the would-be sailors found themselves in the school infirmary, stricken with scarlet fever.

In summer of 1900, Roosevelt entered Harvard University and began his education in public service, social service, politics and government.

In December 1900, James Roosevelt died at age 72. James and Franklin were very close. Sara described the relationship between father and son as one of friends and companions. James frequently had joined Franklin in the search for an obscure or elusive stamp.[4] Franklin, Sara and James are shown in Figure 7 in a circa-1899 portrait.

At Harvard, FDR renewed his interest in stamp collecting and worked on his collection regularly. He also began writing for the *Harvard Crimson* and delved more into social work with a distant cousin, Anna Eleanor, who was from the Oyster Bay side of the family tree.

Figure 7. FDR at age 17, with James and Sara.

CHAPTER 4

Marriage and Early Career

While still at Harvard, Franklin Roosevelt fell in love with Anna Eleanor (better known as Eleanor) Roosevelt. He informed his mother of his intention to marry Eleanor as soon as he graduated and passed the New York bar examination.

In 1904 Roosevelt graduated from Harvard and enrolled at Columbia Law School, where he stayed for two years, long enough to pass the New York bar examination but not long enough to earn a degree. On St. Patrick's Day of 1905, Franklin and Eleanor Roosevelt were married in New York. President Theodore Roosevelt, Eleanor's uncle, gave the bride away. A photograph of Eleanor Roosevelt on her wedding day is shown in Figure 8.

The newlyweds spent the next few months traveling in Europe on their honeymoon. They returned to the United States, where they spent a year sailing, golfing, fishing and relaxing at the family summer home at Campobello, in the Canadian province of New Brunswick.

At about the same time Franklin and Eleanor arrived at Campobello, Sara departed for a trip abroad. Franklin's letters to her show he was again spending more time with his stamp collections.

Figure 8. Eleanor Roosevelt on her wedding day, March 17, 1905.

"August 25, 1907
Mama . . . I have added quite a lot to my stamp collection and would love it if you could bring me the new French stamps and the 2 franc stamp too. Also the higher values of German stamps . . . "[1]

He followed up with a letter to her as she arrived in England in the fall:

> "September 5, 1907
>
> Mama . . . George Clymer and I have bought an old stamp collection and are busy over it. My interest in my collection has really revived! And I find it a pretty good one to use as a foundation. While in England do you think you can get me an unused 1 pound stamp and an unused 10 shillings?"[2]

Later in the fall of 1907, FDR began an apprenticeship as a clerk in the law firm of Carter, Ledyard and Milburn, at 54 Wall Street, where he remained for three years. It was during this time that he became more active in politics.

In 1910, Democratic District Attorney John E. Mack of Dutchess County, in which Hyde Park lay, spoke with FDR at his New York law office. Mack was impressed with the young man and asked Roosevelt to run for political office as a Democrat. FDR accepted the offer.[3]

That year he successfully ran for a seat in the New York State legislature. This was the genesis of his political career. When he departed for Albany to assume his place in the state senate, he took his stamps with him.

During the campaign for re-election to the senate in 1912, Roosevelt was stricken with typhoid fever and could not leave his bedside to campaign. He hired Louis McHenry Howe to write letters, meet constituents and be his eyes and legs. Howe also visited stamp shops around different areas of the state to buy stamps from want lists that FDR had prepared.

Howe's expertise in political campaigning led FDR to a re-election vote that far surpassed his 1910 total. Howe continued to act as FDR's political strategist, best friend and stamp gofer.

Figure 9. FDR as assistant secretary of the Navy with boss Josephus Daniels.

While in the senate, FDR became an admirer of New Jersey Governor Thomas Woodrow Wilson, who was considering a run for president on the Democratic ticket. FDR supported Wilson's bid for the office with such ardor that Wilson offered FDR, through Josephus Daniels (the newly appointed secretary of the Navy), the position of assistant secretary of the Navy. FDR accepted at once:

"All my life I have loved ships and been a student of the Navy," he told Daniels, "and the Assistant Secretaryship is the one place, above all others, I would love to hold."[4] FDR is shown with Daniels in Figure 9.

FDR resigned his seat in the New York Senate and departed for Washington, where he was sworn in as assistant secretary of the Navy on his eighth wedding anniversary, March 17, 1913.

As assistant secretary, he added many covers to his collection, especially covers from foreign lands addressed to him and to the Department of the Navy. It was at this time that FDR began to take more interest in the postal markings that arrived on the mail addressed to him.

Navy business kept FDR busy in the days prior to World War I, and although he saved stamps and covers that came to him, he found it more difficult to find time to mount and write up his new acquisitions.

A letter written to Eleanor Roosevelt in 1916 shows that he tried, whenever possible, to put in a little time with his stamps:

"August 8, 1916

Babs . . . I brought my stamp albums down here and am putting in many which have drifted down to me during the past ten years."[5]

In February 1917, as Germany severed relations with the United States as a prelude to U.S. involvement in the war, FDR was on a Navy inspection tour of Haiti and Santo Domingo. He acquired many missing stamps for his albums during this tour.

He continued to rely on his mother to bring back stamps from her world travels until her death in 1941.

U.S. ambassadors and foreign diplomats within the Wilson administration also were asked to keep an eye out for interesting stamps and covers. In this way FDR was able to amass a vast number of stamps and covers. Figure 10 shows a cover obtained by FDR while he was assistant secretary.

On April 2, 1917, Woodrow Wilson asked Congress to declare war, and on April 6, the United States entered the "war to end all wars."

Certainly FDR's collecting activities were curtailed during this time, but

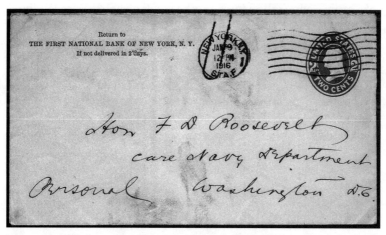

Figure 10. This January 1916 cover addressed to FDR in care of the Navy Department found a place in his stamp collection.

he continued to receive stamps from diplomatic sources worldwide throughout the war.

Roosevelt added to his collection on another inspection trip made in July 1918. This time the trip was to Europe itself. Stops included London, where he talked with King George V. He also visited many of the battlefields throughout France. In Paris he visited relatives, and in Italy he discussed naval matters with the prime minister and the U.S. minister of the Marine.

At the conclusion of the war, he returned to Europe to settle numerous claims against the Navy by private citizens and to dispose of naval property overseas, such as radio towers and other installations.

In late 1919 and early 1920, Roosevelt's name was mentioned on more than one occasion as a possible vice presidential running mate to balance a ticket with a strong Democratic presidential candidate needed to succeed the ill and failing Woodrow Wilson. (Ironically it was first suggested that FDR run with Herbert Clark Hoover, who at that time was undecided on whether he was a Republican or a Democrat.)

Roosevelt was chosen to run with the Democratic nominee James Cox against the Republican ticket of Warren Harding and Calvin Coolidge. Roosevelt and Cox went down to inglorious defeat.

Roosevelt wrote to Cox that he thought it improbable that the Democrats would win the White House again until there was a serious economic depression.[6] With that ominous and fateful prediction in hand, FDR returned to private life, assuming his duties as partner in the law firm of Emmet, Marvin and Roosevelt, which he had helped establish in the spring of 1920. He also accepted a far more lucrative position as vice president in charge of the New York office of the Fidelity and Deposit Company of Maryland, one of the largest surety bonding houses in the nation.

During the first week of August 1921, FDR sailed to the family summer home at Campobello. Following a frantic week of swimming, fishing, hiking and putting out a forest fire with his children and friends, FDR took to his bed with body aches and a temperature of 102 degrees, which his doctor diagnosed as a severe cold.

CHAPTER 5

Illness and Re-emergence

Roosevelt's illness was not a cold. He had been stricken with poliomyelitis, or polio, a virus that attacks the brain and spinal cord and often leaves its victim paralyzed. He was paralyzed from the neck down.

His mother believed he should give up politics and retire to the life of a country squire like his father before him. Relaxing amidst his trees and managing the affairs of the Hyde Park estate tempted FDR. But Eleanor Roosevelt and Louis Howe knew FDR's ambitions and realized he could never be truly happy away from politics and social service. They began a deliberate and ultimately successful campaign to keep him active.

Franklin Roosevelt had three immediate goals following his polio attack. The first was to regain feeling in his body. He recuperated at his summer home at Campobello, shown here in Figure 11. With much hard work, he regained the feeling in his arms and his back in a few months, which allowed him to sit up unassisted. The feeling in his legs never fully returned, and his movement was restricted to a wheelchair or the strong arm of an aide or one of his sons.

FDR's second goal was to convince friends and family, especially his wife and children, that everything would be fine and that they should not worry or treat him any differently. This attitude, begun in the sick bed, would continue to be a mainstay in FDR's philosophy regarding many things in his private and public life.

The third goal, once he returned to New York from Campobello, was to

Figure 11. The Roosevelt summer home in Campobello, where FDR recuperated after his initial polio attack.

spend quality time with his stamps. To disassociate his mind from the terrible pain of the stretching of his atrophied muscles and the agonizing daily massages, FDR retired to the world of stamps. He had time to mount stamps in his albums and make detailed notes now that feeling in his arms had returned.

Howe was again enlisted to aid FDR in his stamp search: "FDR ... missed not being able to attend the various auctions to look for rare stamps . . . so Louis took over this chore, brought catalogs to the bedside, pored over them with FDR, then spent hours in the various auction rooms until he found just the thing that would gladden Franklin's heart."[1]

But Howe was not simply a gofer for FDR. FDR's discourses on stamps,

Figure 12. FDR's friend, campaign manager, secretary, and stamp collecting partner, Louis McHenry Howe.

history and geography had sparked an interest in Howe, and under FDR's expert tutelage Howe became a stamp collector. Louis Howe is pictured in Figure 12.

Throughout the years of FDR's recovery, stamps were at the forefront of his efforts to relax. Since he could no longer hike, golf, horseback ride or do any of the strenuous activities he had done previously, his main avenue of relaxation was to work on his stamp albums or discuss stamps with fellow collectors.

While Roosevelt recovered, Howe kept FDR's name and political philosophies in the newspapers and in front of Democratic politicos. He kept the extent of FDR's illness secret.

Roosevelt appeared in public more often, frequently visiting his New York office of the Fidelity and Deposit company of Maryland.

In 1923 he went on a short sailing excursion with friends and felt refreshed and restored by the voyage. He was convinced that "pulling myself about the decks" helped strengthen his leg muscles, and the adventure culminated in his purchase, along with friend Johnnie Lawrence, of a secondhand houseboat, which they named *Larooco* (for Lawrence, Roosevelt and Company).[2]

The boat gave many hours of relaxation to the sea-loving FDR. He spent hours sitting in the sun on the deck of the *Larooco* working on his stamps.

In 1924 Roosevelt learned of a rundown spa and resort in Georgia whose waters were said to be very buoyant and therapeutic. Willing to take a chance on anything that might help him walk again, FDR went to Warm Springs,

Georgia, and began to make progress in the naturally warm waters that flowed into the spa.

Roosevelt eventually purchased the property and opened its doors to thousands of crippled children and adults who were stricken with polio. Warm Springs became a sanctuary to him. He built a cottage, where he could relax, even during the most difficult times. The cottage is shown in Figure 13.

Figure 13. FDR's cottage at Warm Springs came to be known as the Little White House during his presidency.

CHAPTER 6

Governor of New York

Perhaps nothing personifies Franklin Roosevelt's determination both to recover and to remain a voice in Democratic politics more than his presidential nomination speech for New York Governor Alfred E. Smith at the 1924 Democratic National Convention. Walking unassisted, with only crutches to maintain his balance, FDR shuffled himself agonizingly toward the podium where he put Smith's name into nomination, calling him "the happy warrior of the political battlefield."

Smith lost the nomination to little-remembered dark-horse candidate John W. Davis, but Franklin Roosevelt's position in the party rose considerably that night. The interest generated in Roosevelt led Howe to the conclusion that FDR could be elected president of the United States.

While Roosevelt worked at rehabilitating his legs at Warm Springs, Howe busied himself with keeping FDR's name and views in the minds of the Democratic politicos.

At Warm Springs, FDR's legs improved. In 1926, he purchased the resort at Warm Springs and built a small cottage for himself on the property. By 1927, he turned it into the nonprofit Georgia Warm Springs Foundation. He hired physiotherapists and orthopedic specialists, had a pool enclosed with a glass cover for year-round treatment and opened the former resort as a hydrotherapeutic center for the treatment of polio victims.

He was again called upon to nominate Al Smith for the presidency at the 1928 Democratic convention. This time Smith won the nomination to represent the party in the general election against Republican Herbert Clark Hoover. Smith anticipated a difficult battle. As part of his strategy he wanted a strong Democrat in the governor's office in Albany. FDR fit the profile.

Roosevelt balked at running for governor so soon. Not only did he believe that Hoover and the Republicans would be swept into office, but his own personal strategy called for him to run for governor in 1932, be re-elected in 1934 and then try for the White House after Hoover had completed his two terms in 1936.

FDR agreed to run for governor after John J. Raskob, vice president of General Motors and DuPont, offered to assume the Warm Springs Foundation's financial responsibilities.

FDR's decision to run for governor angered Howe, who felt their carefully laid out plans for FDR's political future had been severely undermined. When Roosevelt received the gubernatorial nomination, Howe immediately fired off a telegram to him at Warm Springs:

"Jimmie Walker nominated you and it was carried unanimously . . . Mess is no name for it . . . For once, I have no advice to give."[1]

Nevertheless, Howe remained at Roosevelt's side to help direct the campaign, hoping to muster enough votes for Roosevelt that his political reputation would not suffer too much after what Howe believed would be an inevitable defeat.

Roosevelt awoke the morning after the election to find the Republicans safely ensconced in the White House and governors' mansions across the nation. He was surprised to learn that he had won the New York gubernatorial race by 25,000 votes.

It was during this first campaign for governor that FDR's interest in stamps began receiving publicity. Until then, most people had no idea that he was a stamp collector. Stamp collecting was looked upon as a child's hobby.

Roosevelt proudly announced that he was a stamp collector and that he had been a collector since he was about 9 years old. He said his stamps were a valuable source of relaxation to him, and that he had learned world history and geography through postage stamps.

Rex Tugwell, Roosevelt's friend and advisor, described FDR's interaction with stamps as such:

"He played with stamps, and in his play learned more than anyone supposed possible. This was the kind of geography that not only places identifiable areas in relation to each other, but assesses their relative importance through historic changes."[2]

When word of FDR's interest in stamp collecting became public, people from all parts of the country began sending stamps and covers to the governor. Shown in Figure 14 is an April 1, 1931, cover sent to Governor Roosevelt from an admirer in South Carolina. It is a Post Office Department first-flight cover commemorating the first airmail flights through South Carolina. A short note with the cover informed FDR that it was the first of a set of four covers marking the flight that the sender had prepared for the governor.

FDR had the mail clerks at the governor's mansion save stamps and covers for him. Shown in Figures 15-17 are but three of the covers from his collection during his years as governor. The Raleigh, North Carolina, cover is interesting in that it comes from Josephus Daniels, secretary of the Navy in the Wilson administration and the man who offered FDR the job of assistant secretary. Daniels had retired to North Carolina, where he ran the *Raleigh News and Observer* newspaper.

One of Roosevelt's sources of stamps in his gubernatorial days was the auction sales of Maxwell Ohlman, a philatelic auctioneer and former president of the American Stamp Dealers Association, who had offices at 116 Nassau Street, New York City.

Ohlman saved much of his correspondence with FDR concerning stamps, and Herman Herst Jr. relates, in his book *Stories To Collect Stamps By*, some of FDR's mail bidding from these auctions.

> "The first of many auction bid sheets which FDR sent to Ohlman . . . was for Ohlman's 106th sale . . . probably sent about August 1928 . . . FDR was assigned the bidder number 126. He bid on seven lots, his highest bid being $2.50, his lowest $1.00."

At this time, FDR was using the address of his office at the Fidelity and Deposit Company at 55 Liberty Street, New York. On December 8, 1928, following the election, Roosevelt wrote Ohlman to thank him for his congratulatory message. He mentioned that he wished he could have a "chat about stamps," but that he was very busy "studying the problems of State Government."[3]

For the June 12-13, 1929, auction Herst relates that the bid sheet "was signed F.D. Roosevelt, Executive Mansion, Albany, N.Y." It has bids on 13 lots, the lowest $1.50, the highest $9.50. Ohlman's notation "unsuccessful on all" is on the sheet.

FDR was more successful in Ohlman's September 30, 1930, auction. Here Ohlman wrote on the bid sheet, "Bought one lot $3.50 plus 10¢ postage . . . Best luck at election . . . M.O." FDR returned payment along with a note reading, "Thanks — things look all right so far! F.D.R."[4]

FDR's total dealings with Ohlman and details on what he purchased will probably never be known. It is clear that FDR did much of his auction business through the dealer.

"I am off to Warm Springs for a three week holiday," FDR wrote to

Figure 14. An admirer from South Carolina sent this first-flight cover, one of a set of four, to FDR as governor of New York.

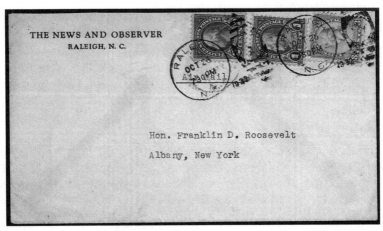

Figure 15. This cover from FDR's collection contained a letter from Roosevelt's old boss, Josephus Daniels, who ran the News and Observer.

Figure 16. This cover from Kennebunk, Maine, was postmarked on election day 1932, when FDR was swept into the White House.

Ohlman on November 13, 1930, "and I am taking my stamps with me."[5]

During FDR's second term as governor in 1931, when plans for his presidential bid were under way, Ohlman wrote to FDR and suggested that membership in stamp societies might help FDR promote his love of stamps to those undecided voters who might be stamp collectors. FDR replied on July 8, 1931:

> "I think it is a very pious idea about my joining the A.P.S. (American Philatelic Society). I am enclosing the application blank duly signed. The address given is my permanent one

Figure 17. This William Penn first-day cover was sent to Govenor Roosevelt by one of his secretaries, Missy LeHand.

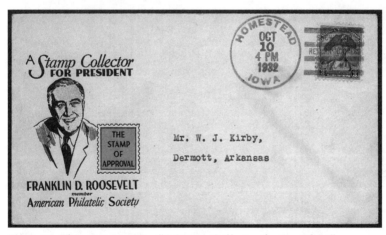

Figure 18. This cover touting "A Stamp Collector for President" was created by the American Philatelic Society.

at Hyde Park. I am inclined to think that one of the societies is enough for me at the present. What I need most at the present time is a month off to play with stamps."[6]

FDR was signed up as a card-carrying member of the APS and given number 11590.

Ohlman's suggestion proved to be a good one. The APS embraced its new member and shortly thereafter envelopes like the one shown in Figure 18 began to appear, touting "A Stamp Collector For President" and featuring a cachet of FDR. Campaign workers used the envelope for mailings, and soon the rest of the country knew of FDR and his interest in stamps.

CHAPTER 7

A Stamp Collector for President

One of Louis Howe's assistants during FDR's gubernatorial campaigns of 1928 and 1930 was James Aloysius Farley, a friendly Irishman from Grassy Point, New York. A consummate political strategist by birth, Farley had a photographic memory for faces and names that would be important to FDR.

When FDR mentioned to the press that he was a stamp collector, Farley, as FDR's campaign manager, immediately took advantage of the statement. He had labels created for use on envelopes that called attention to FDR's hobby and calling for "A Stamp Collector for President." Farley is pictured with FDR in Figure 19.

In the White House, President Hoover seemed dismayed by the fuss being made over FDR's hobby and sought to capitalize on the apparent popularity of stamp collecting.

In 1932, the now defunct Society of Philatelic Americans was holding its convention in Washington, D.C., and President Hoover invited the members to call at the White House for a visit. The president had photographs taken with members and at one point mentioned in an off-hand manner that his entire family had been stamp collectors since they were children.

The philatelic press took an interest in Hoover's remark. They had never heard about anyone in the president's family having an interest in stamp collecting. Research by reporters turned up the fact that some of Hoover's family did indeed collect stamps as children. Evidence also pointed to the fact that Herbert Hoover collected stamps as a child.

Hoover, however, had made an error in mentioning his stamp-collecting past. There followed a spurt of philatelic publicity that Hoover would just as soon not have had happen at all. Most adult collectors felt he was typical of those who considered stamp collecting a child's hobby and something to be outgrown when one reached a certain age. FDR, on the other hand, was proud that he

Figure 19. James A. Farley, at right with FDR, put Roosevelt's hobby of stamp collecting before the public during the 1932 presidential campaign.

23

had collected stamps all of his life.

Members of the press began to question Hoover about stamps and stamp collecting. Collectors wanted to know why stamps were so badly centered? They also wanted to know why the Hoover administration did nothing to repeal the much hated "illustrations law," which prohibited stamp publications, album makers and catalog publishers from illustrating U.S. stamps in their entirety for collector identification.

Hoover had no answers. Roosevelt, however, had definite opinions on stamps and collectors. He too was curious about the number of badly centered stamps being produced and their causes. As for the illustrations law, he quickly, to the delight of stamp collectors all over the world, made known his opinion on the need to repeal such an outdated and silly law.[1]

On election day, FDR soundly defeated the beleaguered Hoover, garnering 57.4 percent of the popular vote. The United States had been in the grip of the Great Depression since 1929 and was ready for a change in the Executive office, so there is no telling exactly how much the stamp-collecting community contributed to FDR's overwhelming victory in November 1932.

When FDR chose his Cabinet and personal staff, he began by naming Howe his personal secretary and presidential aide. He next rewarded James A. Farley with the position of postmaster general.

One of the first things on the new PMG's agenda was the issuance of the first commemorative stamp of the Roosevelt administration. The 3¢ Newburgh Peace stamp commemorated the return to peace after the American Revolutionary War. When dies for the new stamp were made, Farley, knowing of FDR's interest in stamps, took the proofs to the White House and asked FDR if he would like to make the final selection. The president so enjoyed making the selection that Farley decided that FDR would make the final selection for all future U.S. stamps. An example of the Newburgh first-day cover and a letter from FDR to Farley are shown in Figure 20.

Among Roosevelt's other Cabinet appointments was Harold L. Ickes to the position of secretary of the Interior. Ickes, shown in Figure 21, an old Bull Moose supporter of Teddy Roosevelt, was also a stamp collector. Shortly after he was sworn in he searched the archives of his new department for old Interior Department revenue stamps.

His search was successful. He later recalled that when he was with the president on April 1, 1933: "I handed him, 'as one philatelist to another,' a full sheet of one hundred, old three cent Department of the Interior stamps, and a similar sheet of six cent stamps. These have been obsolete for many years, but I had a tip that there were some in existence in the office of the chief clerk and I was lucky enough to get several sheets of each, all that were left. He (the president) was delighted and said that he would frame them. These stamps in sheets are very rare indeed, and I am sure that he was as pleased to get them as I was."[2]

As the new PMG, Farley was invited to the Bureau of Engraving and

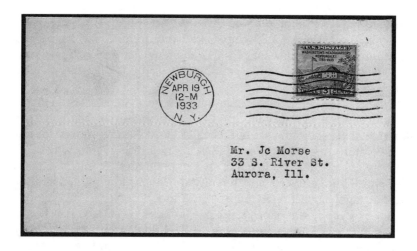

April 20, 1933

Dear Mr. Postmaster General:-

            The item in my
collection which for me will always have
the greatest personal historic interest
is the Newburgh Commemorative Stamp, the
first copy of which comes with your letter
from Newburgh. I shall always remember
that it is the first stamp to be issued
under the administration of my Postmaster
General, to whom I send my affectionate
regards.

                Always sincerely,

Figure 20. The first stamp issued under the Roosevelt administration was the Newburgh Peace commemorative, the first-day cover of which is shown here along with FDR's letter to Postmaster General Farley.

Figure 21. Harold Ickes, shown at left wearing a hat, was FDR's secretary of the Interior and a fellow stamp collector.

Printing to witness the production of the 3¢ Newburgh Peace commemorative stamp. While there, the huge presses were stopped, and the postmaster general purchased a full sheet of 400 of the new stamps for himself and for President Roosevelt. The PMG would do the same for 19 other new stamp issues in 1933.[3]

When news of FDR's interest in stamps spread, interest was rekindled in many thousands of "closet collectors" who had put away their collections as children. A new generation of youngsters began collecting stamps for the first time. Two of the many examples of FDR inauguration covers, which grew in popularity after FDR'S election, are shown in Figures 22 and 23. One man's hobby, and the inner peace and serenity it brought to him, had sparked an interest in stamp collecting in many Americans.

Not everybody was happy with the hub-bub over stamps, however. Actor John Barrymore announced in a May 1933 edition of the *American Magazine* that he hated stamp collectors. When asked the reason, Barrymore replied that when he was in New York, he knew a stamp collector "who was a practical joker, and who one night put ashes in my bed. I have hated stamp collectors ever since."[4]

Young people were especially impressed by FDR and his hobby. During the Depression, when many young people were electing to ride the rails in search of a better life, stamp collecting supplied the spark of interest in many of them to continue their education and spend their free time with stamps instead of on the streets.

One young lady who had collected stamps even before the publicity about FDR's avocation was a Kansas girl in her early 20s named Vonnie Butner. She had been ill and incapacitated for more than 10 years. She nevertheless retained her enthusiasm for education, using stamps and covers to convey that knowledge.

When FDR was elected president, Butner, like many thousands of others, sent him written congratulations. As reported in *Linn's Weekly Stamp News*, FDR not only found the time to reply to her letter, but also sent her a mint copy of a 1929 Italian stamp (Scott 223) featuring the profile of King Victor Emmanuel, which Miss Butner framed along with an autographed photo she had requested of the president. "The President will never know how many happy moments he has provided for that Kansas girl," the article in *Linn's* stated.[5]

FDR was invited to attend the meeting and banquet of the American Philatelic Society in Chicago, Illinois, August 21-26. Also invited by society president Dr. C.W. Hennan were Postmaster General James A. Farley, Interior Secretary Harold L. Ickes, and First through Fourth Assistant Postmasters General Joseph C. O'Mahoney, W.W. Howes, Clinton B. Eilenberger and Silliman Evans. Also receiving invitations were Michael Eidsness, superintendent of the Division of Stamps, and A.W. Hall, director of the Bureau of Engraving and Printing.

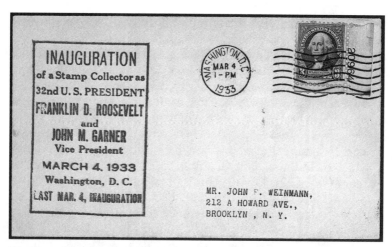

Figure 22. This 1933 inauguration cover, postmarked in Washington D.C., calls attention to FDR's stamp-collecting hobby.

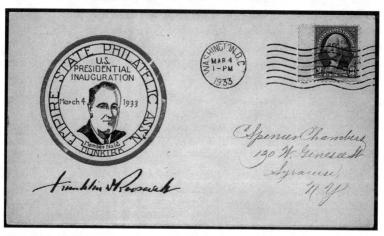

Figure 23. This inauguration cover from the Empire State Philatelic Association boasts FDR as member number 12.

FDR would not be able to attend the meeting personally, but he arranged with PMG Farley to have a special printing of two souvenir sheets to be released in conjunction with the APS meeting. The sheets each contained 25 stamps, one sheet depicting the 1¢ Fort Dearborn stamp (Scott 728) and the other reproducing the 3¢ Federal Building (Scott 729). The sheets were issued imperforate and without gum.

The Century of Progress sheets, Scott 730 and 731, were the first of several souvenir sheets issued while FDR was president and Farley was PMG.

As the president and his staff unveiled the New Deal and their plans for national recovery during that first tumultuous year of 1933, even the stamp-collecting community was called to arms.

An article dated December 2, 1933, *Linn's Stamp News* asked collectors: "Would it not be fitting for our President's fellow stamp collectors to declare Christmas Day of 1933, 'Roosevelt's Christmas?' Let each fellow collector resolve to cooperate for national recovery by making a Philatelic Gift to someone on Christmas Day, 1933. Make some boy or girl yes, man or woman, happy and in this way create additional business, which means more jobs, and give happiness to hundreds of people unknown to you. This will bring true happiness to yourself.

"The greatest results can be obtained through a spontaneous outpouring of cooperation by each and every collector. Do not wait for organized cooperation. Let the collectors of the nation, as individuals, lead the way to National Recovery and show others that they are more than 'stamp nuts.' Other lines will be quick to follow the lead. Do your part today. Act, and then spread the slogan 'Roosevelt's Christmas.' "[6]

CHAPTER 8

What FDR Collected

To describe what FDR did not collect would be a far easier task, and take much less time, than to list the stamps and covers he did collect. Franklin Roosevelt was a stamp collector in the most literal sense. He never referred to himself as a philatelist, only as a stamp collector. He made no bones about his disappointment in seeing a blank space on one of his album pages, and would search far and wide to fill that space.

Although he was reluctant to refer to himself as a philatelist, a philatelist was what he was. He was not merely a casual collector, but a student of the detail and designs of stamps, as well as the history and geography of the country that issued the stamp.

When FDR entered the White House in 1933, he had approximately 20,000 stamp specimens mounted in some 30 albums. Added to this were the thousands of stamps accumulated over the years that he had not found the time to mount or write up. The number of covers the president had would be impossible to determine since he was not one to throw a cover away if it had a stamp, any stamp, attached to it.

One of FDR's finest collections comprised the stamps of Haiti, a collection he started as a child. Many of the stamps were also acquired when he was assistant secretary of the Navy. The earliest Haitian issues were included in the collection, and in 1933 FDR searched for plate blocks for the 1-centime and 2c Liberty Head issues of 1881 (Scott 1-2). Other fine collections consisted of the stamps of Mexico and Hong Kong.

Among the president's other collections were two albums devoted to the stamps of Santo Domingo and one album of stamps from the Danish West Indies. Other volumes contained the stamps of Argentina, Bolivia, Brazil, Chile, Colombia, Costa Rica, El Salvador, Guatemala, Honduras, Nicaragua, Panama, Paraguay, Peru and Uruguay. There were also albums for the Bahamas, Bermuda, Cuba, Puerto Rico, Trinidad, British Guiana, French Guiana and Dutch Guiana, Canada, Newfoundland and Nova Scotia.

During the early presidential years, FDR concentrated on the stamps of North, South and Central America. His hope, like many other collectors, was to complete these collections.

He also had a fine collection of U.S. stamps and covers, which would be added to handsomely during his tenure in office. He had a 12-album collection of what he called "general material" of the 19th and 20th centuries, which included stamps from France, Italy, Germany, Austria, Turkey, China, Japan and the Union of Soviet Socialist Republics.

Figure 24. This cover from FDR's collection was signed by Admiral Richard E. Byrd. It was one of many covers in a three-volume collection.

FDR had an affinity for covers bearing Army and Naval cancellations and postmarks. He had a three-volume collection of covers from government officials, Naval officers, foreign diplomats and a variety of other celebrities such as the Wright Brothers and Admiral Richard E. Byrd. Figure 24 shows a cover sent to FDR. The cover was autographed by Admiral Byrd. The president also collected cancels and postmarks from the U.S. Civil and Spanish American wars, as well as cancellations from various arenas of World War I.[1]

When Roosevelt took office in March 1933, newly appointed Postmaster General James A. Farley gave the president stamps and first-day covers of every U.S. new issue. He even went so far as to see that FDR was supplied with die proofs of U.S. stamps beginning with the 1894 set of regular stamps (Scott 246-63) and continuing through the Newburgh Peace issue of 1933 (Scott 727).

The die proofs would cause some controversy after FDR's death in 1945, but in 1933 no one thought there was much wrong with Farley presenting the die proofs to the president (see chapter 12).

Shortly after taking the oath of office on March 4, 1933, Roosevelt issued a proclamation closing the banks all over the country. After signing the bank holiday proclamation, FDR asked Assistant Secretary of State Wilbur J. Carr to remain in his office after the others had left. He asked Carr if his department received a number of interesting foreign stamps in its daily mail. When Carr replied in the affirmative, FDR said: "I should appreciate it greatly if you would sometimes bundle up a few and send them over to me."

Every Friday, a State Department envelope arrived at the White House with stamps and covers for the president to look through.[2] Figures 25 and 26 show two examples of covers saved by the State Department for FDR.

The mail room at the White House also sent the president any unusual stamps and covers that were addressed to him. The president went through

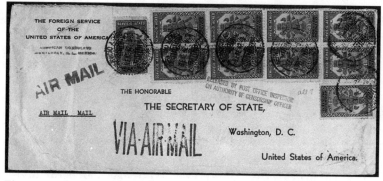

Figure 25. The State Department saved stamps and covers for the president. The one shown here is from the American Consulate in Mexico.

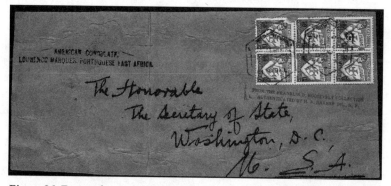

Figure 26. Front of a package from the American Consulate in Portuguese East Africa, saved by the State Department for FDR's collection.

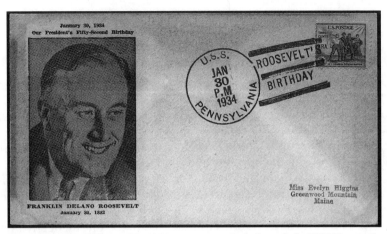

Figure 27. This January 30, 1934 cover canceled aboard the **USS Pennsylvania** *was created to celebrate FDR's birthday.*

these items during any free time he had between appointments, while talking on the phone or before he retired for the evening.

One of the collections begun by FDR in the White House, and one which gave him the most pleasure, was a collection of covers addressed to him in strange or interesting ways. Covers with artistic renditions of the president or fancy calligraphy and ornamentation that caught his eye found their way into this collection.

His favorite items in this collection were what he referred to as his "bouquets and brickbats." These were covers addressed to him in very unusual ways. In the area of "bouquets" were covers simply addressed "My Friend," "The Greatest Man in the World," "The Man Who Saved Our Farm" and "God's Gift to the U.S.A."

In the area of "brickbats" were covers addressed "Dishonorable Franklin Deficit Roosevelt"; "Rattlesnake Roosevelt"; "Chief Shooter at the Moon, White Father of the Pretty Bubbles"; "Benedict Arnold 2nd"; and "F.D. Russianvelt."

Inauguration covers canceled in cities all over the United States were popular items sent to FDR. Also birthday covers postmarked on the president's January 30 birthdate were often received at the White House. An example is shown in Figure 27. Many collectors, knowing the president's love of the Navy, had covers postmarked on board U.S. naval vessels on his birthday. Collectors prepared sets of three birthday covers from the towns in Minnesota named Franklin, Delano and Roosevelt. A set of these covers is shown in Figure 28.

Franklin Roosevelt also kept a number of stamps and smaller collections presented to him by foreign dignitaries, ambassadors and world leaders. Figure 29 shows a small album of Yugoslavian stamps presented to FDR by Peter II. Interior Secretary Harold Ickes relates how a meeting between FDR, Ickes, Treasury Secretary Henry Morgenthau Jr. and Soviet Commissar of Foreign

Figure 28. These covers, postmarked in the Minnesota towns of Franklin, Delano and Roosevelt, were popular gifts to the president by fellow collectors on his birthday.

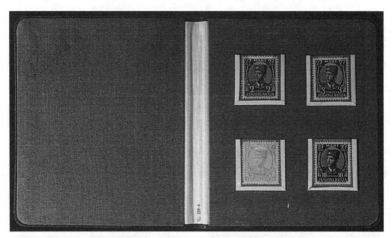

Figure 29. A small presentation album of four Yugoslavian stamps signed and given to Franklin Roosevelt by King Peter II.

Affairs Maxim Litvinov and his aide Constantin Oumansky turned from politics to stamps. The meeting was scheduled to finalize plans for U.S. recognition of the Soviet Union in November 1933.

"At the end of the Luncheon," Ickes wrote in his diary, "an interesting thing occurred. Mr. Litvinov put his hand into an inside pocket of his coat and pulled out a couple of booklets of Russian stamps which he proceeded to show to the president. On Mr. Oumansky's right was Henry Morgenthau Jr., who remarked to Mr. Oumansky that I (Ickes) was a stamp collector too, whereupon he also drew out several booklets of Russian stamps which he handed to me for my inspection, later making me a gift of three of the booklets. They are all new issue stamps, some of which have not yet reached this country. Mr. Litvinov gave the president the stamps he had been showing him and Mr. Oumansky also gave some to Mr. Morgenthau, whose son is a collector.

"Mr. Oumansky told me that he collected stamps and he also confided to me that Mr. Litvinov was a secret, but passionate collector. According to his story, Mr. Litvinov does not advertise this hobby. On one occasion Mr. Oumansky called at his home and found him behind a closed door. He (Litvinov) kept him waiting until he could put all of his stamps away so that he wouldn't be caught at it."[3]

Christmas seals also formed a part of FDR's collection. On December 8, 1933, Dr. Kendall Emerson, managing director of the National Tuberculosis Association, arrived at the White House with several association delegates to present the president with a collection of Christmas seals. The collection comprised blocks of four of all seals issued from 1907 to 1933. A few perforation varieties were represented by single labels when blocks could not be located. Complete booklet panes of three, six and 10 seals were also included. For each year all types, perforations, printers marks, essays, proofs and progressive color proofs were also included.

The collection comprised 77 pages of seals mounted and written up. Emerson left the White House expressing his hope that the president would enjoy the seal collection, whereupon FDR replied, "I will take it to bed with me tonight."[4]

Many nations gave FDR presentation albums of stamps or framed copies of special issues they thought might appeal to or have special significance to him. Nineteen such collections were donated by FDR to the Roosevelt Library between 1941 and 1945 as follows:

1. Portfolio of stamps from 11 American republics issued in commemoration of the 50th anniversary of the Pan-American Union. The stamps were presented to FDR on June 26, 1940, as a gift of the ambassadors and ministers of American republics.

2. A collection of 23 commemorative stamps issued by several American republics depicting acts of American friendship. The collection was autographed by the foreign ministers of the issuing nations and presented to FDR by President Vargas of Brazil during the Rio de Janeiro Constitution meeting in April 1942.

3. A block of ½-penny Australian stamps presented in a frame to FDR by D.R. Sparks of Armcliff, New South Wales, in 1941.

4. An album of 10 Brazilian stamps issued at various times from 1890-1940 in commemoration of the Pan-American Union. This was a gift of President Vargas of Brazil.

5. Set of four Chinese stamps issued in connection with the sesquicentennial of the U.S. Constitution (Scott 364-67) mounted in a small buckram album.

6. A similar set of Chinese stamps not mounted in an album.

7. An album of various stamp issues from the Dominican Republic given to FDR by President Trujillo Molina in December 1935.

8. A sheet of 3½-markka stamps issued to commemorate the settlement of Finnish immigrants in the Delaware River Valley (Scott 214). This was a gift of President Kallio of Finland.

9. An album containing 12 die proofs and three pages featuring 42 regular and airmail French stamps. This was a gift of the French Embassy.

10. Four sheets of four stamps each, issued by Guatemala in commemoration of the 150th anniversary of the U.S. Constitution (Scott C92). This was a gift of the president of Guatemala.

11. An album of native stamps from Haiti, created by Leon Montes and presented to FDR by Haitian president Stenio Vincent in April 1934.

12. Six stamps from Mexico in a leather album with photographs from which the stamps were made and issued in connection with the opening of the Mexico City-Nuevo Laredo Highway in 1936 (Scott 725-27 and C77-79). This was a gift of Mexican President Cardenas.

13. An album containing a complete set of 1939 Will Rogers airmail stamps

from Nicaragua and the photographs from which the stamps were made (Scott C236-40). This was presented by Nicaraguan President Somoza.

14. A small album containing a complete set of the then-current stamps of the territory of Sarawak and inscribed "From Their Highnesses, the Rajah and Ranee of Sarawak to Franklin D. Roosevelt, President of the United States of America."

15. An album of mint and canceled-to-order stamps from the Soviet Union in commemoration of the participation of the USSR in the New York World's Fair of 1939.

16. A U.S. first-day cover from 1940 featuring the 3¢ Emancipation Proclamation stamp (Scott 902). This was a gift of D. Fabian of Portland, Oregon.

17. A single U.S. Printing Tercentenary stamp of 1939 (Scott 857) in a gold frame. This was presented to FDR by Farley on February 17, 1940.

18. A framed picture of the White House and the president, surrounded by U.S. Presidential stamps of 1938, and several commemorative stamps issued during Roosevelt's administration.

19. Two sheets containing 76 local stamps from Hamburg in varying degrees of imperfection, issued between 1858 and 1860. The sheets were a gift of Peter Gunter of Little Rock, Arkansas, in June 1934.[5]

FDR's interest in stamp collecting was a worldwide advertisement for the hobby, and many stamp dealers sent items to the president in thanks for his having revived interest in the hobby. Hugh M. Clark, treasurer of the Scott Stamp and Coin Company of New York, sent FDR a copy of the 1935 Scott catalog with the following note:

> "Dear Mr. Roosevelt:
>
> "It is with pleasure that I am sending you under separate cover a copy of the new edition of our catalogue which I trust may be of some interest and use to you.
>
> "I trust you will accept it as merely a token of our deep appreciation of the benefits you and your efforts have brought to the stamp collecting hobby."[6]

As president, FDR continued to submit bids to Maxwell Ohlman on Nassau Street, but no longer made out his bid sheets by hand or even signed them himself. His 1935 bid sheet was typewritten, and the name was simply given as "The President, The White House." FDR was successful in this bid, purchasing seven lots of stamps totaling $45.75.

Other members of FDR's inner circle also wrote to Ohlman when they were looking for something specific. Howe once wrote to Ohlman to inquire about purchasing 19th-century stamps for one of his collections. He wanted the stamps to be poor, cheap copies, explaining that he wished to fill those annoying blank spaces at a cheap price and then gradually replace them with better copies as his budget allowed.

In April 1935, FDR told his secretary, Missy LeHand, that he wanted blocks of four of the soon-to-be released British King George V Silver Jubilee stamps. LeHand asked Ohlman if he could procure a set of blocks for the president. Ohlman ordered a set from Whitfield King and Company of Ipswich, England, at a cost of $30, to which he added the cost of the draft and postage, and billed the White House for a total of $32.25.

Secretary of the Interior Harold L. Ickes contacted Ohlman on December 3, 1935, when he was shopping for the president's Christmas present:

"I wonder if you know President Roosevelt's stamp collection well enough to tell me what he is chiefly interested in, and whether there are one or two stamps that he would like to have. I have in mind to buy him a stamp or two for Christmas of a total cost not to exceed $50.00."

Ohlman answered with a letter the next day informing Ickes that FDR usually bid on stamps from Jamaica and Hong Kong, and that he was also looking for missing rarities like Scott 9, 10, 15a and 16 for his Argentina collection.[7]

During World War II, FDR renewed an interest he had started earlier, that of collecting covers and cancellations from Army Post Offices located in the war arena, as well as ship cancels from interesting ports. He made detailed notes of where the APO cancels were from and what type of military engagement was taking place there at the time the letter was posted.

For his U.S. collection, FDR purchased full sheets of stamps issued during his tenure and had them autographed in the selvage by himself, members of his Cabinet or other politicos and personalities who had some connection with the event or person depicted on the stamp. He did the same for first-day covers whenever possible. A good example is the Baseball Centennial stamp of 1939 (Scott 855), issued at Cooperstown, New York, on June 12, 1939, in conjunction with the opening that day of the Baseball Hall of Fame and Museum. Many outstanding baseball celebrities were in attendance that day to witness the induction of Lou Gehrig into the Hall of Fame. PMG Farley made sure that many of the players signed the front of FDR's first-day cover before he took it to him at the White House. A fine example of a cover signed by FDR is the 1932 Winter Olympic Games FDC shown in Figure 30.

In 1933, in conjunction with Admiral Richard E. Byrd's second Antarctic Expedition, a U.S. stamp was contemplated to help defray the costs of the expedition. FDR approved a stamp that would bear a 25¢ denomination, with a percentage going to the Post Office Department and the remainder going toward paying the cost of transporting the covers to Byrd's Antarctic base camp at Little America for cancellation for collectors.

When PMG Farley brought four horizontal designs to the White House for FDR's approval, the president vetoed all four. He picked up pencil and paper and sketched a rough idea for a vertical stamp depicting a map of the world and a group of lines, representing the various routes Byrd had taken in both his air and ground expeditions over the frozen continent. His sketch is shown in Figure 31. Roosevelt decided that the stamp would bear a 3¢ denomination, but would sell for 53¢, the difference going to the expedition.

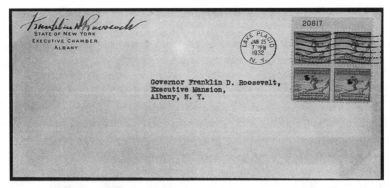

Figure 30. 1932 Winter Olympic Games first-day cover signed at upper left by FDR who opened the games as governor of New York.

Figure 31. When the sketch of the Byrd stamp was presented to him, FDR noticed a misplaced line denoting one of Admiral Byrd's polar routes so the president sketched his own design.

The Bureau of Engraving and Printing produced the stamp according to FDR's sketch, and the first sheet of Byrd stamps was removed from the press at the Bureau, autographed by Admiral Byrd and presented to the president in October 1933.

The Byrd stamp (Scott 733) was the first stamp designed by FDR. It would not be the last. During his administration, he would personally sketch designs for the 1934 Mother's Day commemorative (Scott 737), 1934 airmail special delivery stamp (CE1), 1936 Susan B. Anthony commemorative (784), 1937 Virginia Dare issue (796), 1938 6¢ airmail stamp (C23), 1939 Statehood anniversary stamp (858) and the 1940 Defense Trio (899-901).[8] (See *Franklin D. Roosevelt and the Stamps of the United States 1933-1945.* Linn's Stamp News 1993)

Roosevelt was also the recipient of many elaborate stamp collections that were already arranged, mounted and written up by others. While he enjoyed looking over them and learning from them, he usually relegated these to his home at Hyde Park. His enjoyment of stamp collecting came from handling, arranging, mounting and writing up his own stamps.

Distinguished philatelist Ernest A. Kehr, who often visited FDR at the

White House to discuss stamps, wrote that FDR never allowed anyone to touch his albums or to mount his stamps. FDR told Kehr: ". . . Working on the stamps myself provides all the fun of the hobby, so why should I let anyone enjoy it for me?"

Kehr went on to say that FDR's album pages were filled with pencil notations that showed the thoroughness with which each stamp was studied by the president. A stamp with a partial cancellation was mounted in an album in such a way that FDR could draw or write in the missing portion of the cancellations. Also if a stamp was already represented on a page and FDR received another with a different postmark or that was a shade variety, he would mount the new one beneath the first. Some stamps in FDR's collections were represented by as many as 50 specimens.

Shortly before FDR's death in April 1945, he remarked to Kehr that he had become interested in collecting field markings and censorship cachets applied by military postal authorities in all parts of the world. Since most cancellations of this type included only a date and an APO (Army Post Office) or FPO (Fleet Post Office) marking, designed to protect the secrecy of the outfit that used it, FDR reveled in being able to puzzle out and identify the geographic location from which a letter was sent.[9]

After FDR's death, many people were surprised to learn that interwined among the gems of FDR's collections were many stamps that could be referred to as seconds. Poorly centered, badly perforated, thin, creased and heavily canceled stamps all found a home in FDR's collection. As Kehr explained, FDR was not subject to "conditionitis." "He regarded every stamp in his collection as a source of information about the country or the peoples by which it had been issued."[10]

It was FDR's attitude toward stamps and what they represented that made him America's number 1 stamp collector. That attitude, according to Farley, helped bring the number of stamp collectors in the U.S. from two million in 1933 to over nine million by 1938. Farley also opined that stamp collectors accounted for philatelic sales increasing from $300,000 in 1933 to over $2 million annually by 1938.[11]

CHAPTER 9

FDR's Stamps as Educational Tools

From his earliest years as a stamp collector, Franklin Roosevelt did more than just acquire stamps and mount them in his album. He studied stamps. He made it a point to learn not only about the country that issued a stamp, but the local area as well. He learned who or what was depicted on a stamp, and why that person, place or event was being honored. He discovered the political or sentimental reasons behind the stamp, and the controversy and problems that followed the issuance. Stamps were not only a hobby to help him relax, but a source for information and learning that remained with him all his life.

"I don't know anybody," Eleanor Roosevelt told a meeting of the Westchester County League in Rye, New York, on August 4, 1934, "who knows so much history and geography as my husband, and I think that is largely due to his interest in stamps."[1]

One example of FDR's sense of geography is the time an Egyptian collector showed him a cancellation from Sohag and asked if the president had ever heard of the area. He was stunned to discover that FDR knew all about Sohag, even remarking to the collector that Sohag was only five miles southwest of Akhimim, which, he pointed out, was another rare cancellation from the area.[2]

FDR's acute sense of history and geography stood him in good stead when he approved U.S. stamp designs. When the proof for the 1933 Byrd Expedition issue (Scott 733) was brought to FDR for final approval, the president remarked that the line representing Byrd's New York-to-Ver Sur flight aboard his plane *America* was not correctly depicted. "He landed further north than that," Roosevelt told the Bureau representative who had brought the proof to him. Further investigation proved the president correct, and the more precise route was re-engraved in time for the October 9, 1933, release date.

For the 25¢ Transpacific airmail stamp (Scott C20) issued in November 1935 to carry mail across the Pacific Ocean, the Bureau of Engraving and Printing created a stamp depicting the *China Clipper*, the plane used to fly transpacific mail. Also depicted in the background were four ships that had been used to transport mail in the past, a Chinese junk, a Yankee Clipper, a 19th-century steamship and a modern oceanliner.

When the proof was brought to FDR, he immediately pointed out that the very small rendition of the Yankee Clipper on the left side of the stamp was engraved with only two masts on her instead of the correct three. Chances are not many people would have noticed the missing mast on the small rendition of the ship on the stamp, but FDR did, and it had to be corrected. Bureau engravers immediately went to work to add the missing mast to the stamp.[3]

FDR's historical sense again came to the rescue in 1938 when the Post Office Department issued a single stamp to honor the sesquicentennial of the first settlement of Swedish colonists at Wilmington, Delaware (Scott 836). After the proof was shown to FDR, the third assistant postmaster general returned post haste to the Post Office Department. "Hold everything," he said to his superiors, "the Chief says this design must be changed to include the Finns, because they were among these first colonists who landed on 'The Rocks' at Wilmington, Delaware."[4]

Although time was short, the die was re-engraved to include the Finns before the stamp was issued on June 27, 1938.

FDR insisted that U.S. stamps be checked and double checked for accuracy before they were issued.

For the 125th anniversary of the first steamship crossing of the Atlantic Ocean by the ship *Savannah*, he approved a suggestion to depict the *Savannah* at sea. The *Savannah* was a unique ship in that her smokestack, instead of going straight up, was bent at an angle toward the rear of the ship so that the smoke trailed behind the ship as she sailed (see Figure 32).

On April 26, 1944, after looking over the design for the stamp, FDR penned a memo to PMG Frank Walker, cautioning him to make sure that the smokestack was depicted in the correct manner. He also noted that the U.S. flag on the ship was shown with 20 stars and wondered whether a 21st star for Illinois, which had entered the Union in 1818, had not been included on the U.S. flag by the time of *Savannah's* voyage.[5]

The PMG went to work and reported back to FDR on May 4, 1944.

". . . Be advised that Captain Dudley Knox, U.S. Navy, has been con-

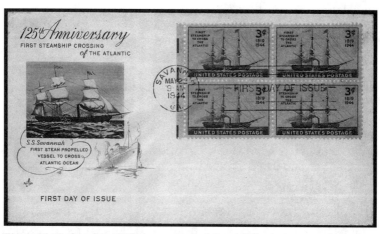

Figure 32. Only when FDR was satisfied that all depictions on the steamship Savannah *were historically correct was the stamp approved.*

Office of the Postmaster General
Washington, D. C., 25

Memorandum to the President.

S. S. Savannah Stamp

Referring to your memorandum of April 26, please be advised that Captain Dudley Knox, U. S. Navy, has been consulted and he has confirmed the authenticity of the break in the smokestack shown on the model for the Steamship stamp procured from the detailed description of the S. S. Savannah by J. B. Marestier. Also, he believes other details of the design correctly depict a ship of the period. He has, therefore, initialed the design as having his approval. Therefore, authorization has been given the Director of the Bureau to proceed with the engraving of this stamp.

As completed, 20 stars will appear on the flag at the top of the foremast. With regard to the flag, as you will recall, although Illinois, the twenty-first State, was admitted into the Union in the preceding December, the law did not permit the inclusion of the twenty-first star in the flag until July 1, 1819.

Figure 33. This Post Office Department memo to FDR assured the president that all depictions he had questioned had been checked and confirmed.

sulted and he has confirmed the authenticity of the break in the smokestack shown on the model . . . Also, he believes other details of the design correctly depict a ship of the period.

"As completed, 20 stars will appear on the flag . . . With regard to the flag, as you will recall, although Illinois, the twenty-first State, was admitted into the Union in the preceding December, the law did not permit the inclusion of the twenty-first star in the flag until July 1, 1819."[6]

A first-day cover of the Savannah stamp is shown in Figure 32. Walker's memo is shown in Figure 33.

One historical error that managed to get past FDR occurred on a stamp from a set personally requested by him to honor U.S. Army and Navy heroes (Scott 785-94).

The 4¢ Army issue (Scott 788) depicted Southern Civil War Generals Stonewall Jackson and Robert E. Lee. FDR approved the models for all the stamps in the series, but his eagle eye failed him.

After the stamp was issued on March 23, 1937, the Post Office Department and Bureau of Engraving and Printing received many angry letters, especially from the Southern states, complaining that General Robert E. Lee had been depicted with only two stars on his shoulder. Since Lee was a three-star general, many felt that the omission of a star was a deliberate slight by the Post Office Department to the great Southern hero.

The Post Office Department conceded that a star was somehow lost in the transition from design to engraving, but that it was not intended as a slight to General Lee. The Robert E. Lee stamp is shown in Figure 34.

Figure 34. The 4¢ Robert E. Lee stamp was the one stamp with a historical error to slip by Roosevelt's eagle eye for accuracy.

During World War II, FDR's interest in stamps, geography and history would emerge several times and prove that the president's stamps had indeed taught him well.

When Roosevelt requested that a map room be set up at the White House so that he could follow the progress of troops and ships, his Naval aide, Captain John L. McCrea, set to work. McCrea was astounded by FDR's knowledge of the geography of the world, especially the little-known regions. McCrea was amazed that FDR "knew so much about an insignificant lake in a small foreign country." Roosevelt explained to McCrea that this was what happens "if a stamp collector really studies his stamps."[7]

During a 1942 meeting at the White House of the members of the Allied Pacific War Council, which consisted of FDR and the leading representatives of nations at war with Japan, a proposal was made by New Zealand Deputy Prime Minister Walter Nash that Allied forces capture and occupy a small South Pacific Island as a stepping stone in the drive toward Japan. "That would be all right," FDR said, "but the Island of Mangareva would be better." Nash replied that he was embarrassed to admit he wasn't acquainted with Mangareva. "Oh, it's in the Tuamotu Archipelago, in the postal administration of Tahiti," replied FDR. "I know the place because I am a stamp collector." Shortly afterward, Allied forces moved onto Mangareva.[8]

FDR never stopped learning and acquiring knowledge from stamps. He was never too busy to inquire about a stamp or a postmark that caught his interest, and took the time, usually before retiring for the evening, to jot down what he had learned next to the stamp in his album.

When they learned of his stamp collecting interests, many national leaders sent stamps to FDR. Most were surprised when FDR began to discuss the stamps and the history behind them as if he had been a fellow countryman instead of a foreign leader. Chinese president Chiang Kai-shek was so impressed by FDR's knowledge of his country's history that he presented FDR with a complete set of all Chinese stamps issued since the Republic of China was founded in 1912.

Perhaps Roosevelt's greatest historical coup using the postage stamp as his weapon came in January 1943, when the president was encamped in Morocco's seaport city of Casablanca for war-strategy conferences with British Prime Minister Winston Churchill.

Long before this meeting took place, FDR and Churchill had been trying to secure the cooperation of the various French Freedom Fighters who had been fighting not only among themselves, but were also firing on Allied troops in many arenas since France had fallen in 1940.

Trying to alleviate these problems, FDR chose not to recognize the leadership of self-proclaimed Free French leader Charles de Gaulle. He preferred for the time being to maintain relations with the Vichy regime of Marshal Henri Petain in hopes that he might be able to prevent the French fleet from being turned over to Hitler.

In 1942 the next item on the Allied agenda was the invasion of North Africa. Called "Project Torch," the North African invasion would depend on the acquiescence of the French in a coordinated landing that would place troops from all of the Allied nations on the African continent.

Roosevelt began to look for a French leader who had an allegiance to Vichy and who could command the French forces in North Africa when American troops landed. To this end he selected General Henri Giraud, a popular French resistance fighter who had been in command of the French 7th Army when the German offensive opened in May 1940. After the 7th Army collapsed, Giraud was taken prisoner and interned in the castle of Konigstein in Saxony. From there he escaped in April 1942 and returned to Vichy France. Giraud was smuggled out of France by submarine and arrived in North Africa a few days before Project Torch got under way.

The relative ease of the Allied landings was also helped by a cease-fire order given by French Admiral Jean Darlan, which stopped French units from firing on landing troops. Giraud agreed at the time to command French troops while Darlan controlled the civil government. This clandestine shuffling left Charles de Gaulle out in the cold.

This shuffling also put FDR in the position of having to deal with Darlan, one of the most notorious Nazi collaborators. Roosevelt insisted that dealing with Darlan would help secure North Africa in less time and with fewer casualties. He would continue to deal with Darlan as long as necessary to achieve that goal.

On Christmas Eve 1942, a 20-year-old French monarchist assassinated Darlan. FDR responded by elevating General Giraud to head the civil war as well as military affairs in North Africa. This infuriated de Gaulle, who did not like the idea of Giraud rivaling him for what he perceived as his rightful place as leader of the French Resistance.

It was amidst these troubles that FDR departed for Casablanca in January 1943. Among the topics he and Churchill needed to discuss was the need for cooperation between Giraud and de Gaulle.

Roosevelt believed Giraud was willing to compromise, but that de Gaulle was preoccupied with his political future at a time when his energies should have been directed toward the need for complete military victory.

At Casablanca, Churchill and FDR decided that Giraud and de Gaulle should share power. Both French generals were summoned to Casablanca for a conference. Giraud arrived promptly, but de Gaulle waited two days. While awaiting de Gaulle's arrival, FDR amused himself with the stamps that he

Figure 35. Argentina Scott 416 gave FDR the idea to unite two feuding French generals during World War II.

had brought to Casablanca. When a member of the president's party went to FDR's room one day, he found the president studying a stamp with an unusual intensity. The stamp was an Argentine stamp (Scott 416) whose vignette included a pair of clasped hands holding a staff surmounted by a Cap of Liberty, such as the ones worn by the French Revolutionaries in 1789. FDR showed the stamp to his visitor saying, "I suspect that here we have the operation for Giraud and de Gaulle." The stamp is shown in Figure 35.

When de Gaulle finally arrived minutes before a press conference was scheduled to begin, FDR persuaded de Gaulle and Giraud to step outside with him and Churchill for a photo session. After a few group shots were taken, Roosevelt requested that photographs be taken of de Gaulle and Giraud shaking hands, a request neither of the Frenchmen could veto with the eyes of the world's press upon them. The result was one of the most famous World War II photographs. The photograph is shown in Figure 36.

Giraud and de Gaulle held a meeting of their own, which culminated in a short communique announcing their tenuous alliance. Although no real agreement was reached between the two French generals, the meeting had the effect that FDR desired. An idea spawned by a stamp had set aside the egos of de Gaulle and Giraud long enough to get on with the business of the war.[9]

Figure 36. Generals de Gaulle and Giraud shake hands in the famous World War II photo.

CHAPTER 10

FDR and his Fellow Stamp Collectors

By the time Franklin D. Roosevelt entered the White House on March 4, 1933, his hobby of stamp collecting was well-known to most of the American people. A special relationship developed between the president and the stamp-collecting community. Figure 37 shows an airmail cover sent to FDR by a postmaster whose office straddled the states of Arkansas and Texas.

Franklin Roosevelt's unabashed love of stamps prompted many closet collectors of the time to proudly announce that they were stamp collectors. Thousands of new collectors caught stamp fever from the president. As a result, stamp shops opened all over the country. This interest prompted many of the large-city newspapers to begin or enlarge their coverage of new stamp issues or stamp events. Papers that had never had a stamp column were now devoting as many as two pages to the hobby in their Sunday editions.

Figure 37. This cover was sent to FDR by a postmaster whose post office straddled the border between the two states of Arkansas and Texas.

Circulation, newsstand sales and advertising of the philatelic press soared in the 1930s. Collectors frequently wrote to stamp publications asking questions, seeking advice on stamps and products, and, above all, making suggestions for stamps.

The Post Office Department and Bureau of Engraving and Printing received tremendous amounts of mail from citizens who wrote to make suggestions for new stamps.

The White House mail room was inundated with letters from people asking about the president's collection, suggesting stamp ideas, inviting FDR to attend local stamp shows and bourses, and asking FDR to send them stamps from his collection.

Roosevelt's relationship with his fellow collectors went further than correspondence. The president helped promote and advertise the hobby, to get others interested in stamps, and to make the hobby more interesting and accessible to a more diversified group of people.

Many children wrote to the president to ask about his stamp collection and request stamps so that they could begin a collection. At first, FDR's secretaries wrote to the children and explained that the president couldn't fill their requests. Later, FDR asked the staff in the mail room to clip stamps from incoming mail and make up small packets of stamps. To these were added the foreign stamps from the State Department that the president did not keep for his own collection. Letters to children changed from apologies for not being able to supply stamps to letters like the following:

"March 23, 1944

PRIVATE

My dear Bobbie:

The President has received your friendly little letter of March nineteenth and, in compliance with your request, he is very glad to send you the enclosed stamps for your collection.

I also have pleasure in sending you the President's very best wishes for your welfare and happiness.

Very sincerely yours,
Grace G. Tully
Private Secretary"[1]

The very essence of this letter shows the remarkable relationship between FDR and young collectors. Although the letter was written by Grace Tully, FDR had paved the way for stamps to be sent to these children. The PRIVATE at the top of the letter and the best wishes from the president gave the letter a personal touch. This letter is shown in Figure 38.

Many curious children also wrote to the White House to find out what kind of stamps the president collected. In February 1935, one of FDR's secretaries, Marvin McIntyre, asked the president for a short paragraph about his stamps that could be used to answer a letter from a boy who had written to the White House (see Figure 39).

Figure 38. The president's secretary, Grace Tully, answered many letters written by children to the president about his hobby. Tully gave each letter a personal touch.

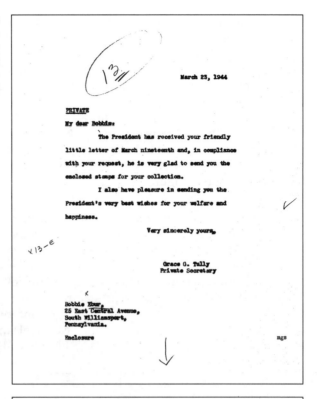

March 25, 1944

PRIVATE

My dear Bobbie:

The President has received your friendly little letter of March nineteenth and, in compliance with your request, he is very glad to send you the enclosed stamps for your collection.

I also have pleasure in sending you the President's very best wishes for your welfare and happiness.

Very sincerely yours,

Grace G. Tully
Private Secretary

Bobbie Ebur,
25 East Central Avenue,
South Williamsport,
Pennsylvania.

Enclosure   mgs

Figure 39. Another secretary, Marvin McIntyre, went directly to the president for a paragraph he could send to inquiring children.

THE WHITE HOUSE
WASHINGTON

February 6, 1935.

MEMO FOR MAC

Write him and say that there is not very much to write about the President's collection except that it is a fairly large one and was becoming so voluminous that in recent years the President has specialized more and more in West Indies and Central and South America, and that he has been adding to his collection ever since he was about eight years old.

F. D. R.

"Write him," the president wrote, "and say that there is not very much to write about the President's collection except that it is a fairly large one and was becoming so voluminous that in recent years the President has specialized more and more in West Indies and Central and South America, and that he has been adding to his collection ever since he was about eight years old. F.D.R."[2]

Missy LeHand, FDR's private secretary, had already become adept at answering children's letters inquiring about FDR's stamps. She had been his secretary since 1921. LeHand was able to provide more specific information about what FDR collected, as evidenced by this February 27, 1935, letter to a young collector (see Figure 40):

> "My dear Paul:
> Replying to your letter of February twentieth, addressed to the President, I am very glad to give you the information you desire. The President began collecting stamps when he was about eight years old. He specializes in the stamps of Haiti, Santo Domingo and Hong Kong, and his collection now consists of about ten thousand stamps.
> Very sincerely yours,
> M.A. LeHand
> PRIVATE SECRETARY"[3]

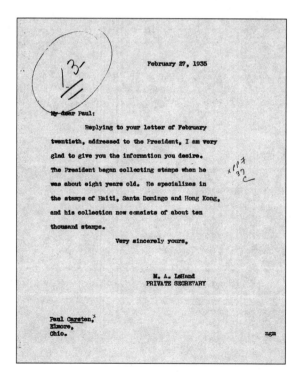

Figure 40. FDR's secretary, Missy LeHand, provided children with a little more statistical information about the president's collection.

Figure 41. FDR and his three secretaries. From left, Missy LeHand, Marvin McIntyre and Grace Tully.

The three secretaries are shown with FDR in Figure 41. Even though the replies were necessarily short and concise, each child received an answer to his letter to the president of the United States.

FDR received gifts of stamps and covers. Figure 42 shows an example of a reply by presidential secretary Missy LeHand to a letter and cover sent to FDR from a fellow collector during National Airmail Week in 1938. The sender requested that the envelope he used to send FDR the cover and letter be returned to him.[5]

Some people wrote to FDR in the hope of getting the president to become a philatelic pen pal, something that would have been impossible for him with his busy schedule. Others wrote for basic philatelic information, like the man who penned a letter to the president in October 1934 asking FDR if he would please do him the favor of looking up the 1925 2¢ Norse American stamp in his Stanley Gibbons catalog since he could not afford a catalog. He received a letter from LeHand dated October 11, 1934, advising him of both the Stanley Gibbons number and price for the stamp (Scott 620).[6]

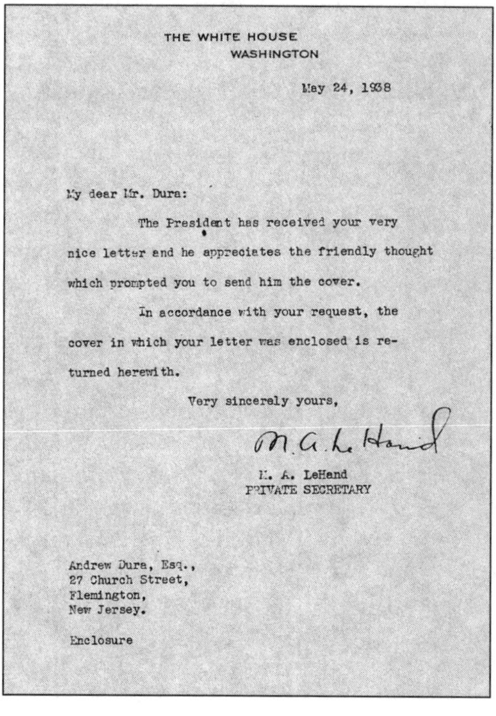

THE WHITE HOUSE
WASHINGTON

May 24, 1938

My dear Mr. Dura:

The President has received your very nice letter and he appreciates the friendly thought which prompted you to send him the cover.

In accordance with your request, the cover in which your letter was enclosed is returned herewith.

Very sincerely yours,

M. A. L. Hand

M. A. LeHand
PRIVATE SECRETARY

Andrew Dura, Esq.,
27 Church Street,
Flemington,
New Jersey.

Enclosure

Figure 42. This reply by Missy LeHand acknowledged the receipt by FDR of an airmail cover sent to him by a collector in New Jersey.

51

Roosevelt recommended collecting to anyone who asked about the hobby or expressed an interest in learning more about stamps.

In 1936 FDR's former law partner, Basil O'Connor, told the president that his daughter was thinking of collecting stamps and asked FDR's advice on what sort of stamps she might start with. Roosevelt replied to O'Connor with a note from the White House:

> "I think it a grand idea that Sheelagh wants to become a philatelist. First of all, you should know how to pronounce this.
>
> "Second, as one of the earliest stamps collectors in the world's history, I suggest to her that she start in by specializing. In the old days so few stamps had been issued in all the world that one could collect generally. Specializing means choosing anything from one country up to a dozen, or a continent. It is my thought that:
>
> "(a) Europe is too dull.
>
> "(b) Too many people collect United States stamps.
>
> "(c) The British colonies offer a rather high-priced field.
>
> "Therefore, if I were starting over again I think I would choose either South America or something like French colonies, or Dutch colonies. Or Sheelagh could take some one country like Cuba, Haiti, or Santo Domingo."[7]

President Roosevelt also recommended stamp collecting to Virginia Senator Carter Glass as a possible cure when Glass expressed concern over his son's bout of insomnia.

FDR had interested Farley and both his children in the hobby, and he had won over Louis Howe in his New York senatorial days.

One person FDR doggedly try to get interested in stamps, but never could, was his friend Secretary of the Treasury Henry Morgenthau Jr. In the selvage of many sheets of U.S. stamps from FDR's collection can be found the autographs of FDR and Morgenthau. "I send him a full sheet of stamps every time a new one is issued with a note that it's for his collection," FDR told philatelic writer Ernest Kehr. "But that fellow just takes the stamps, says thank you, and puts them aside. Someday I'll make a stamp collector out of him yet." Morgenthau is shown with FDR in Figure 43.

FDR had packets of stamps sent to people who were bedridden. Mrs. Padgett of the White House mail room was also asked to regularly send stamps to Ernest A. Kehr, national chairman for Stamps for the Wounded, which supplied wounded servicemen with stamps and supplies during their recuperation. Every week a package of stamps and covers weighing about 20 pounds arrived at Kehr's office. The memo shown in Figure 44 was taken from FDR's files one week before his death in 1945. It informed the president that the latest batch of stamps had been sent.[8]

One of the most disheartening things about being confined to Washing-

*Figure 43. Secretary of Treasury Henry Morgenthau Jr.
is shown in the automobile with FDR.*

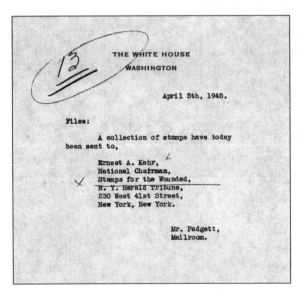

*Figure 44. A weekly memo
from the White House mail
room informed the president
that a package of stamps
had been sent to Stamps for
the Wounded.*

ton and to a wheelchair for FDR was his inability to attend stamp shows. To
mingle with other collectors, discuss stamps, history and geography, and to
look at what others were collecting was something FDR was unable to do.

In 1935 he was invited to attend the 50th annual APS convention in Washington, D.C. Unable to attend in person, he sent a welcome message to the
society and its members on July 3, 1935:

"TO THE MEMBERS OF THE AMERICAN PHILATELIC

SOCIETY

"It is a pleasure to extend a welcome to fellow members of the American Philatelic Society on the occasion of the Golden Jubilee Convention.

"I feel that the choice of the Nation's Capital for the celebration of this auspicious meeting was well conceived, since in this city more subjects of interest to stamp collectors have been centered than in any other.

"The original painting depicted on the two cent Columbian issue, for example, hangs in the Capitol, the Ericsson Memorial, unveiled by the Crown Prince of Sweden and shown on a recent commemorative stamp, stands along the bank of the historic Potomac within full view of the noble Lincoln Memorial reproduced on our one-dollar stamp. Charles A. Lindbergh's special plane, the Spirit of St. Louis, the Great Seal of the United States shown on the 16 cent Special Delivery Air Mail stamp, the White House and of course the Capitol itself, are likewise to be seen here.

"The Bureau of Engraving and Printing, where the stamps are printed, and the Post Office Department with its new Philatelic Museum opened by Postmaster General James A. Farley will be of interest to you, as well as the Pan American Union where so many international topics which ultimately reflect themselves in the stamps of our Hispanic neighbors are discussed, and the Library of Congress with its wealth of Philatelic lore, will in years to come, linger with you as treasured memories.

"To revel amid these and other philatelic features, I bid you hearty welcome to the Nation's Capital."[9]

The president also received requests to exhibit portions of his collections at stamp shows. Although he exhibited on occasion at national shows, he more often had to turn down such requests. In early 1936, Ohlman inquired of FDR whether he would exhibit some of his stamps at an Atlantic City, New Jersey, stamp show. FDR replied to Ohlman with the following letter dated February 12, 1936:

> "I wish much that I could send some of my stamps to the Atlantic City Stamp Show. I have such an enormous number of requests from stamp clubs all over the country that I have to say 'no' and to confine myself to occasional National exhibits. I know you will understand."

For National Stamp Week, celebrated in November of 1937, the president penned a letter dated November 5, 1937, to Elmer Stuart, president of the Central Federation of Stamp Clubs in Chicago, Illinois:

"Stamp collecting is one of those hobbies which pays an ever increasing dividend. I believe the collector's interest whether he is eighteen or eighty becomes keener every year he follows this pursuit. As one who knows all the delights of collecting I send hearty greetings to the Central Federation of Stamp Clubs and trust the forthcoming observance of International Philatelic Week will serve the happy purpose of acquainting new followers with the compensations which the creation of a collection brings."[11]

President Roosevelt occasionally donated something from his personal collection as an award for a winning exhibition in the youth division of a national show. For the APS convention in 1938, in New Orleans, Louisiana, a youth exhibit was staged in which winners from local APS chapters competed. President Roosevelt donated an autographed page from one of his albums to be presented as the grand award to the national winner of this junior exhibit.[12]

The letters FDR probably most enjoyed were those suggesting subjects for stamps. One of the first stamps issued during his first term was the Mother's Day commemorative of 1934 (Scott 737-38). Its genesis was a simple request in April 1933 by a fellow collector asking if a stamp could be issued to honor American artist James Abbott McNeill Whistler on the 100th anniversary of his birth in July 1934. (For more information see *Franklin D. Roosevelt and the Stamps of the United States, 1933-1945,* by Brian C. Baur. Linn's Stamp News 1993.) The stamp and memo are shown in Figure 45.

Postmaster General Farley said he often brought stamp requests to FDR. In 1935, shortly after the Supreme Court found FDR's National Recovery Act unconstitutional, Farley received a request from a strong anti-New Dealer who "wrote in and suggested that I was so prolific at putting out new issues, why not put out one commemorating the Supreme Court's decision overturning the NRA. I slipped this one in along with the rest and said nothing. The President came across it, chuckled, and said, 'All right. I'll draw you a picture of sick chicken.' "[13]

The following are a handful of examples taken from the pages of *Linn's Stamp News* of interesting requests sent to the White House for FDR.

In 1934 Marion F. Peters of Plainview, Texas, suggested that the "Post Office Department recognize the Cattle Industry by issuing a stamp with a typical cattle brand as the design." The *Linn's* article stated that Mr. Peters "has the largest collection of cattle brands in the world," and had made arrangements to design a layout for a cattle brand for submission to the Post Office.[14]

The acting postmaster of Pasadena, California, proposed in 1935 that a stamp commemorating the Concord Stagecoach be issued and that a memorial trip be made from the East to the West carrying mail "like the old days." The postmaster revealed that his uncle, one of the last surviving stagecoach drivers, still had a coach on his ranch in Walnut, California.[15]

Figure 45. A 1934 Mother's Day first-day cover and the memo that prompted the stamp's release.

Also requested in 1935 was a stamp reproducing a mural depicting the birth of the Star Spangled Banner, which had recently been installed in the Hotel Rennert in Baltimore, Maryland.[16]

In 1940, pharmacists and the chiropodists petitioned for recognition on U.S. stamps. The pharmacists wanted a stamp issued in 1940 honoring the 120th anniversary of U.S. pharmacopoeia. Petitions for such a stamp were to be found at nearly every drugstore counter in the country, and patrons were asked to sign the request for the stamp. The chiropodists, or podiatrists, started a similar campaign in their offices seeking a stamp honoring the centenary of chiropody, which was founded in Boston, Massachusetts, in 1840.[17]

Two of the more interesting collector requests were made during FDR's years in office. The first opined that all stamps should be imprinted with their appropriate Scott catalog number on the back for easy identification. The second, made in 1934, was that the Post Office Department produce "dummy stamps." These stamps, issued in the various shapes of other U.S. stamps, would be used to fill an album space, especially where a collector had a first-day cover of a stamp and did not want to have to purchase another stamp to fill the album space for that issue.

Although requests like these were rejected by either the president or the Post Office Department, many collector ideas and suggestions resulted in issued stamps. Public requests were often the catalyst for stamp clubs, newspapers and even members of Congress to endorse suggestions for the issuance of certain stamps.

An individual request for a stamp honoring Commodore John Barry, who commanded the U.S. Navy's first flag ship *Black Prince*, was made in 1935. It was Barry and his ship that captured the British war vessel *Edward* in 1785. The *Edward* was the first ship to be taken by the Navy of the Continental Congress.

The suggestion caught the fancy of FDR, who kept it in the back of his mind and built upon it until it eventually evolved into the 1936-37 Army-Navy series (Scott 785-94) issued to commemorate nine outstanding members of each branch of the armed forces throughout the history of the United States, from the Revolution to the Civil War.

Public requests also culminated in the Susan B. Anthony issue of 1936 (Scott 784), the 50th Anniversary of Statehood issue of 1939 (Scott 858), the Presidential definitive series of 1938 (Scott 803-34) and the Famous Americans series of 1940 (Scott 859-93).

In regard to the 1938 Presidential series, many had written to the Post Office Department and FDR requesting that a new definitive series be issued to replace the old set of 1922-25 stamps (Scott 551-73).

At FDR's request, the Post Office Department sponsored a contest in which 1,122 sketches were submitted for the George Washington stamp of this series. A design by Elaine Rawlinson of New York City was selected as the best. Rawlinson's original sketch, shown in Figure 46, met with such approval by the selection committee that every stamp in the series was modeled after her original design with no added ornamentation.

Roosevelt enjoyed taking any opportunity to discuss stamps with fellow collectors. Ernest Kehr would fill the bill on those rare occasions when he would visit the White House, and Max Ohlman, through his auctions and correspondence with FDR, would swap stamp stories and information. Un-

Figure 46. Elaine Rawlinson's design of the Washington stamp for the 1938 Presidential series was the winner of a stamp-design contest and became the basic design for all the stamps in the series.

fortunately Roosevelt seldom had time to discuss stamps. Through the letters and suggestions of his fellow countrymen and stamp collectors he was able to stay abreast of current trends in stamps, to monitor the thinking of people with regard to U.S. stamps and to retain a place in the minds of those people as a fellow stamp collector.

CHAPTER 11

FDR's Stamps and Therapeutic R&R

If there was one thing that President Franklin Delano Roosevelt did not have in his days in the White House, it was time enough for rest and relaxation. He could not stop his duties for any appreciable length of time. He took an occasional cruise or fishing trip, but during these excursions, he could never be out of sight of the Secret Service or the press boat that followed him. He also could not travel anywhere where Congress could not reach him with legislation.

His retreat at Warm Springs, Georgia, was no different. During his stays at the resort, he was questioned daily by the members of the press corps. He received visitors and handled routine matters of State just as he did at his desk in the White House. Even though the cottage at Warm Springs had been built with rest and relaxation in mind, it's easy to see why it earned the name "Little White House."

How did he manage to escape the press corps, Congress and the people who simply had to speak to the president? What could he do to free his mind?

Figure 47. Franklin Roosevelt, magnifier in hand, examines a stamp from one of his many stamp collections.

The answer is stamps. Stamps were the only avenue of relaxation that the press corps, Congress and the mail pouch could not encroach upon. The only people who could encroach upon this time were other stamp collectors like Louis Howe, Interior Secretary Harold Ickes, Ernest Kehr or Maxwell Ohlman. To FDR, conversing about stamps with someone knowledgeable on the subject was as great a joy and just as relaxing as mounting them in an album.

It was only at these times that he was able to put everything else aside for a while and unwind. He is shown working with his stamps in Figure 47.

"When I was living at the White House," FDR's son James wrote, "I made it a practice to drop in to see father before retiring. Often I would find him sitting up late at night, working on his beloved stamps . . . "[1]

In his bed for the evening, FDR knew that he would not be disturbed by anyone unless an emergency arose requiring his immediate attention. He was able to spread his albums about him and look over his stamps. With magnifying glass, tongs and hinges on the bedside table, FDR was able to spend quality time looking over his stamps, mounting the new ones he had acquired and making notations alongside the stamps in his albums.

This time with his stamps seemed to rejuvenate FDR in a remarkable way. It was said that sailing on the ocean or the Potomac River would put a healthy glow on FDR's face and a sparkle in his eye that physically showed the rest and relaxation he had gotten from the trip. But the time for sailing excursions were few and far between. With stamps, FDR could recharge his batteries, even if only for a few precious minutes every night before retiring.

Franklin Roosevelt's White House physician, Vice Admiral Ross T. McIntire, wrote of his association with the president:

> "In the beginning of our association I had urged rest periods, but I soon discovered that what refreshed him most was not a discontinuance of activity, but a change of pace. His stamp collection was easily his favorite relaxation from strain.
>
> " . . . I think it is safe to say that there was not one day, even during the war years, when he did not give half an hour to his stamps. Usually after he retired and just before turning out the lamp . . . I remember particularly, he found his greatest relief from fatigue by working away at his albums at the end of an exhausting day . . . A hobby of course; but someday a treatise is going to be written on the therapeutic value of hobbies."[2]

Mentioned in Chapter 8, was the presentation album of Christmas seals given to the president. His comment after receiving them was "I shall take them to bed with me tonight." No doubt the president spent a quiet evening looking over the collection, noting the perforation and color varieties as well as the color trial proofs.

On January 20, 1937, the night of his second inauguration, FDR retired to his study earlier than usual. Knowing that the president was exhausted from the various activities he had dealt with that day, his staff left him alone to rest. At 9:30 p.m., his press secretary Stephen Early peeked in FDR's door to make sure that all was well with the president. "Guess what I'm doing?" FDR greeted him. "Stamps?" Early guessed. "That's right!" FDR replied, engrossed with one of his albums.[3] Figure 48 shows Latvian stamps from FDR's collection.

Ernest Kehr wrote that FDR "devoted a definite period of time to stamps as regularly as to his meals, usually a half hour at night before he switched off his light. It was a tranquil period. The counterpane was dotted with stamps, and the president, propped up on his pillows, lost himself in the peculiar bliss

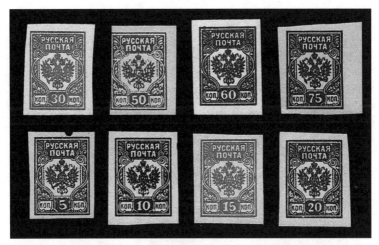

Figure 48. Stamps from Latvia that were part of FDR's collection.

of the hobbyist as he fixed the bright pieces of paper in his albums . . . In Mr. Roosevelt's case, the stamp collecting habit was without a doubt mental therapy of the highest order.

"Mr. Roosevelt's presidency was crammed with vital matters of national and international concern. Yet, busy though these kept him, there were few philatelic activities which did not attract his personal attention. He admitted that he not only read the magazines of the societies of which he was a member, but always followed the stamp columns of his favorite newspapers on Sunday mornings before breakfast was served to him."[4]

But bedtime was not the only time that FDR had with his stamps. Every free minute he had he looked over covers, cut out stamps, separated and sorted packets of stamps and got stamps ready for mounting in his albums.

When FDR was governor of New York in 1930, one of his assistants watched in awe as he took an important call at his desk while at the same time he cut out stamps from envelopes, sorted them into individual piles and made a few notes on a pad of paper.

The same held true when FDR entered the White House in 1933. On one occasion that year he had finished a conference with a group in his office and was expecting another group to follow immediately. The next group, however, was late arriving. His secretary, thinking that FDR was probably angry at the delay, opened the door to the president's office to find FDR sitting at his desk, peering through his magnifying glass at a half dozen or so stamps spread out before him. For several minutes the secretary watched the president examine the stamps, totally oblivious to the fact that he was being watched. Without revealing himself, the secretary closed the door and left FDR to his stamps. When the second group finally arrived, the secretary escorted them into FDR's office. They found FDR putting the stamps in a drawer and look-

Figure 49. FDR signs a sheet of U.S. stamps in his office.

ing totally refreshed and relaxed from the few minutes he had spent with his collection.[5]

FDR sometimes invited stamp collectors and philatelic writers to the White House to discuss stamps when his schedule was light. He sometimes left other people waiting while he and his visitor discussed stamps. Kehr recalled one time while he was at the White House talking with FDR, labor leader John L. Lewis lingered in the waiting room for over a half hour while FDR discussed with Kehr the differences between postmarks on Palestine's first issue.[6] Roosevelt is shown in Figure 49 signing a sheet of stamps in his office.

All aspects of stamps and stamp collecting served FDR in his quest for relaxation. When Postmaster General Farley visited the White House in the early days of the New Deal in 1933, he sat for an hour while FDR discussed and drew a sketch for the commemorative stamp that would be issued in October 1933 in honor of Admiral Richard E. Byrd's Antarctic expedition. He was struck by how stamps helped FDR relax.

"The one thing that impressed me most," Farley said, "was the fact that with the entire country whipped up to a fever of excitement over the National Recovery Act (NRA), the Agricultural Adjustment Act (AAA), and the other policies of the new administration then being put into effect, the president was able to put all those things out of his mind while he sat working at his hobby."[7]

As the world braced for war in the late 1930s and early 1940s, Roosevelt carried a great burden. He not only had to deal with domestic issues in the United States, but much of the now war-torn world looked to him and the

United States to save democracy from the clutches of fascist terrorism.

Even before the United States entered the war on December 8, 1941, FDR had added a grueling travel itinerary to his already full schedule. He visited industrial plants in all parts of the nation, as well as army training camps, Naval installations, shipyards and munitions plants. He traveled tirelessly in an effort to convince Americans that the United States must be prepared to get involved in the war to save democracy.

No matter where he was headed, whether it be to visit the Boeing airplane factory in Seattle, to launch a new ship at a Naval shipyard on the east coast or to visit for a few days with his fellow polio patients at Warm Springs, FDR always took along his stamps. His secretary Grace Tully wrote that "always before a trip he set aside time to collect his stamp paraphernalia, which he neatly packed in a square wooden box which accompanied him everywhere . . . If he planned a trip on Thursday or Friday, he would remind me to call the State Department and ask for the weekly quota (of stamps) to take with him."[8]

When the tide of the war began to turn in favor of the Allies, FDR found himself making a number of trips overseas to discuss war strategy with other world leaders. His stamps always went with him. While preparing for his trip to Casablanca to discuss war strategy with British Prime Minister Winston Churchill in January 1943, FDR told his valet to make sure to pack several of his albums, even if they displaced a few extra changes of clothes that might be needed in the warm climate of Morocco.[9] The Casablanca conference was scheduled to last 11 days, and FDR did not want to be without an adequate number of stamps to tide him over between talks.

His wooden case loaded with stamps and albums also accompanied him to war conferences in Cairo, Egypt, where he met with Churchill and China's Generalissimo Chiang Kai-shek from November 22-26, 1943, as well as the next hop to Teheran, Iran, from November 28-December 1, 1943, where he and Churchill met for the first time with the Soviet Union's leader Joseph Stalin.

By fall 1944, FDR's wooden case had begun to split from years of use and thousands of miles of travel. Grace Tully suggested that he replace the wooden box, but "it wasn't easy to sell the Boss ideas about replacing any article he had grown used to." Tully then asked FDR what she should tell people who called her to ask what the president might want for Christmas or his birthday in January. She later recalled asking, "Would you like a larger case? You seem to have outgrown this size and in leather instead of wood? 'That would be grand' was FDR's answer."

Tully suggested this to Mrs. Vincent Astor, a friend of the president who had been inquiring about what to get him for Christmas. "I gave her specifications and a description," wrote Tully. "But this was not a standard article. She had to have it made to order." The case would not be ready in time for the president's final wartime trip to Yalta to discuss with Churchill and Stalin the final strategy for ending the war. "During the war years . . . it took an age to get delivery on goods of all kinds, and FDR never received his new case. The wooden box made the last overseas trip."[10]

The last of FDR's trips was a much needed vacation to Warm Springs, after his return from Yalta and his report to Congress on the meetings.

A haggered and listless FDR arrived at Warm Springs on March 30, 1945. His staff and members of the press corps were startled by the gaunt and uninterested look on the president's usually animated face. But all agreed that after a few days of relaxing at his cottage with his friends and his stamps, FDR would be back to his old self gain.

The president posed for artist Elizabeth Shoumatoff, who was doing a portrait of him. The portrait is shown in Figure 50. Shoumatoff relates that she had a difficult time getting the sparkle in FDR's eye that she, as well as all of America, had become accustomed to. "So I started a conversation about stamps. I had sent letters to my family that morning and was quite interested in the new Florida three hundredth anniversary stamp and told him about it. I asked him if he, in any way, participated in the design of the stamp and he said that he did, and added, 'Wait 'till you see the new San Francisco stamp, with the United Nations.' He was looking forward to seeing it, and I understood how interested he was in this whole project . . . In a little while . . . a familiar expression began to show. But it was not quite the look I was accustomed to during the past few days. The president seemed so absorbed, with the papers or something else, that when he would look up at my request, his gaze had a faraway aspect and was completely solemn."[11] First-day covers for the Florida Statehood and United Nations issues are shown in Figure 51.

On April 12, 1945, FDR made his last official directive as president of the United States. It should come as no surprise that it concerned stamps. This final directive was to

Figure 50. The unfinished portrait of Franklin Roosevelt that was being painted by Elizabeth Shoumatoff when FDR was stricken on April 12, 1945.

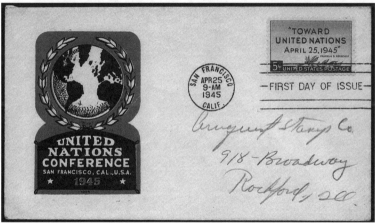

Figure 51. First-day covers of the Florida Statehood and United Nations Conference stamps. These were the last stamps of the FDR era.

approve the design for the United Nations stamp (Scott 928) and to make arrangements with Postmaster General Frank Walker to purchase the first sheet of the stamp when it was issued at San Francisco on April 25 at the first meeting of the U.N. delegates.

A half hour later FDR was stricken with the cerebral hemorrhage that would end his life.

When his personal belongings were gathered up for the last trip to Washington, the stamps he had been working on that morning were among them. In a wire basket on a desk were envelopes and booklets of stamps ranging from recent issues of Romania and Norway to stamps of the Philippines under Japanese occupation. Stamps from a dozen or so other countries were also in the basket, as well as an envelope full of duplicates on which the president wrote "To give away." Along with the usual items found in a stamp collector's arsenal, magnifying glass, scissors, tongs, pads and pencils, a number of small glassine envelopes and a package of stamp hinges, there inexplicably rested in the wire basket FDR's draft card, which he had removed from his wallet and tossed in the basket sometime during his final visit to Warm Springs.[12] FDR's grave in the Rose Garden at his Hyde Park home is shown in Figure 52.

Figure 52. FDR's final resting place in the rose garden of the house where he was born in Hyde Park, New York.

CHAPTER 12

Something for Everybody:
the Roosevelt Stamp Auction 1946

The world was shocked and dismayed by the sudden and unexpected death of Franklin D. Roosevelt on April 12, 1945, at his cottage in Warm Springs. The man who had brought America through the Great Depression and had led the nation, and much of the world, in the battle to defeat fascism and totalitarianism would lead no more. At the threshold of final victory, a massive cerebral hemorrhage removed him from the slate of men and women who would decide the future peace and security of the world.

As Roosevelt was being buried in the rose garden of the Hyde Park estate where he was born 63 years previous, crews were hard at work removing 12 years of his accumulated wealth of collections from the White House.

The president's accumulation of items was indeed a vast one. But he had prepared for removal of his things well in advance of his death. In 1939 Roosevelt deeded the land of his family's estate to the U.S. government as a National Historic Site, and began construction of a library to store his personal and presidential papers after he left the White House. It was Roosevelt's idea that future scholars might wish to study his papers and those of other key New Deal officials to see the thinking that went into dealing with a depression and a world war.

The library also included a museum in which would be placed many of FDR's accumulations. His collections of Naval ship models, paintings, books, birds and thousands of gifts sent to him by both fellow countrymen and by countless world leaders would find a home in the museum. His automobile, manufactured with hand controls so he could drive himself over the many acres of the estate, as well as ice boats he had used to skim over the frozen Hudson River as a child were also ensconced in the museum.

After his death, Roosevelt's cluttered White House desk was moved to the museum and set up with everything in place as it was on the day he died. His lucky campaign hat and his famous Naval cape, which was easier for him to wear than a coat, also were removed to the museum for display.

One of Franklin Roosevelt's collections that did not finally repose in the library or museum was his famous stamp collection. Since none of FDR's children or grandchildren had expressed interest in stamp collecting, the executors of Roosevelt's estate, James Roosevelt, his eldest son; Basil O'Connor, the president's former law partner; and family friend Henry Hackett decided to sell FDR's stamps at public auction so others might have the opportunity to own something from the president's collection.

The executors contacted the New York offices of H.R. Harmer Inc., international stamp auctioneers based in London, England. Roosevelt's collection was to be disposed via public auction to be held in New York City at the earliest possible time. On December 7, 1945, the executors gave final authorization to Harmer to proceed with the sale with the following letter:

> "December 7, 1945
>
> Dear Sirs:
>
> Confirming our earlier correspondence and discussions with O'Connor & Faber, Esqs., this will authorize you to proceed with the disposal of the personal stamp collection of the Late President Roosevelt in accordance with the various proposals heretofore approved by us."[1]

Harmer officials sifted through the massive array of stamps, covers, albums and supplies that made up Roosevelt's collection. Aside from the many collections splendidly written up and contained in albums, there were also many cardboard boxes filled with stamps both on and off paper, stamp packets, sheets and covers numbering in the many thousands. These boxes of items showed two things quite plainly: 1. that FDR saved any stamp that came his way and caught his eye; 2. that FDR never had the time he so desperately craved to go through his stamps and place them in albums.

On December 18, 1945, Basil O'Connor wrote a short foreward as a way of explanation to be included in the auction catalogs when the sale finally took place:

> "In offering the late President Roosevelt's Stamp Collection to the public by sale at auction, it is the purpose of the Executors of his Estate to make the stamps available to the many persons desiring to secure some of those stamps for their own collections. The real satisfaction to be derived from stamp collecting is in possessing and handling the stamps themselves. Much of the true appeal is lost when a collection is withdrawn from circulation and placed on display in a museum merely to be looked at under glass. Viewing the Stamp Collection which Mr. Roosevelt acquired during his lifetime, not only as an Executor of his Estate but as a friend of many years, I am quite sure that he would want to share the very real pleasure he derived from handling his stamps with as many of his fellow collectors as possible.
>
> "Shortly after Mr. Roosevelt's death the Executors received many offers of assistance and advice from collectors and philatelic organizations throughout the country. The preponderance of opinion was that the most satisfactory method of disposing of the Stamp Collection would be by sale at auction. It is hoped that through the medium of these sales, all those

philatelists desiring to acquire items from the Franklin D. Roosevelt Collection will have the equal opportunity of doing so in the true democratic fashion.

"I wish to take this opportunity of personally thanking the many friends and stamp lovers who have contributed their advice and assistance in making the Stamp Collection available to stamp collectors everywhere."[2]

As the Harmer staff went through FDR's stamps, they came to the inescapable conclusion that some of the boxes of stamps and covers would have to be sold as they were. There were simply too many stamps in these boxes to separate and categorize. They also realized it would take several sales to dispose of the massive amount of stamps in Roosevelt's collections. The company arranged an appropriate schedule.

The first sale would take place in three sessions beginning Monday evening, February 4, 1946, at the Parke-Bernet Galleries located at 30 East 57th Street in New York City, adjacent to the Harmer offices. The first session would deal exclusively with FDR's U.S. collection of die proofs, autographed mint sheets and 1934 imperforates of original printings given to him by Postmaster General Farley.

The second session, scheduled for Tuesday afternoon, February 5 at 2 p.m., would feature full, uncut sheets of original U.S. stamp printings as presented to Roosevelt by Farley, as well as the president's general collection of U.S. regular and airmail stamps; first day covers; battleship covers; U.S. local, Official, revenue and encased stamps, telegraph stamps and Christmas seal presentation collections; Confederate States issues; and U.S. possessions. The second session would close with the beginning of the sale of the president's Latin American presentation collections.

The third session, held Tuesday evening at 8 p.m., would feature the president's general collection of all Latin American nations with the exception of Venezuela, which was held over for the second sale. Also featured in the third session would be a selection of albums and binders from FDR's collections.

The second sale was scheduled for Monday and Tuesday, April 1-2, 1946, in three sessions. The sessions were given Harmer International sales numbers 16208, 16209 and 16210. U.S. sales numbers were 308, 309 and 310. The first session, to be held April 1 at 8 p.m., would feature FDR's collection of Venezuela and a number of presentation albums from around the world. The second session, to be held April 2 at 2 p.m., would feature the president's general collection of worldwide stamps. The final session, held at 8 p.m. April 2, would feature FDR's collection of the stamps and covers of Hong Kong, which was started by his grandfather and mother and finally given to him when he was 10 years old. Many stamps of nations in the British Commonwealth also would be featured, as well as miscellaneous stamps, binders and philatelic literature in the president's collection.

Harmer officials announced that public exhibition of the stamps for the first sale would be held at the Parke-Bernet Galleries daily, except Sunday, from 9:30 a.m. to 5:30 p.m., beginning Wednesday, January 30, and concluding just prior to the start of the auction on Monday, February 4.

Auction catalogs were printed for the first three-session sale. The sessions were designated as Harmer International sales numbers 16198, 16199 and 16200. The American sales numbers were 298, 299 and 300. Catalogs were priced at $1.50, which included a copy of prices realized mailed later to each catalog purchaser.

Eleanor Roosevelt wrote the foreward to the catalog, which summed up her husband's love for stamps and the stamp hobby:

> "I am very glad to write a short foreward to go with this booklet on my husband's stamp collection. He derived so much pleasure and relaxation from working with his stamps, I feel rather sad that he never had the time to develop in any of his children or grandchildren the same interest and love for stamp collecting that he had himself.
>
> "This collection is largely valuable because my husband started it as a very small boy, and then acquired a collection which belonged to his mother, much of which was given her by her uncle who had traveled widely in the days when few people traveled. After that start, everything my husband did, everywhere he went and every position he held, served the purpose of increasing his collection since he never forgot this hobby of his which filled a great many leisure hours.
>
> "It had its serious purpose, however, in that through it he learned the most extraordinary amount of geography and history and never forgot any item that he learned. He knew where all of the small islands were that our men had to occupy in the Pacific, and I doubt that most of us in this country ever heard of the great majority of them. He knew the history of far flung places and somehow through his long association with stamps, he had absorbed a world picture which included a knowledge of birds and beasts and agriculture and weather such as few of us have.
>
> "Whether this collection is sold intact or broken up, I hope that whoever acquires the stamps will acquire with them some of my husband's interest and power to lose himself in the occupation of the moment, which is the secret of complete relaxation. These stamps gave my husband great pleasure and I hope they will continue to bring pleasure and good luck to those who may handle them in the days to come."[3]

The Harmer auction catalogs also included two special notes to collectors and bidders. The first informed bidders that the auctioneers felt that many people "would like a lasting record that the original album sheets, on which many of the larger lots are still mounted, came from the collection of the late President Roosevelt. The first note stated: "The Auctioneers have therefore prepared a small rubber stamp and will be pleased to stamp album sheets and lot sheets in the margin, or wherever desired. Out of town bidders are asked to mark their bid sheets if they wish their album sheets and lot sheets to be so stamped. The stamp reads as follows: FROM THE FRANKLIN D. ROOSEVELT COLLECTION AUCTIONED FEB., APRIL, 1946, BY H.R. HARMER INC., N.Y."

The second note informed potential bidders that a special card portraying President Roosevelt examining his collection, with a space beneath it for mounting several stamps, had been prepared, and that such a card would be presented to all successful bidders.[4]

Prior to the first sale, the Roosevelt collection was appraised at $80,000 by George B. Sloane in *Stamps* magazine. (We can assume this appraisal was made in regard to the stamps and covers as described in the first two auction catalogs only and did not include the cartons of stamps that had not been sorted.) Catalogs were mailed, and the stamps for the first sale were put on public display for potential bidders to see prior to the actual sale. All was in order for the first sale on February 4, 1946.

The Storm Before the Calm

When auction catalogs for the first sale began reaching collectors, an immediate upheaval occurred, rocking not only the philatelic establishment in the United States, but also affecting millions who had no special interest in stamps. The problem concerned die proofs that made up the first session and the first 140 lots of the auction.

After Roosevelt had taken office in 1933, the Post Office Department and Bureau of Engraving and Printing began presenting him with progressive die proofs of the stamps being issued under his administration, beginning with the Newburgh Peace issue of 1933 (Scott 727).

FDR was pleased with these souvenirs, so the Post Office Department and Bureau of Engraving and Printing presented him with a collection of die proofs of all U.S. stamps produced by the Bureau of Engraving and Printing beginning with the inaugural 1894 series of 13 regular stamps from 1¢ to $5 (Scott 246-63) and continuing up to the Century of Progress stamps of 1933 (Scott 728-29).

At the time, no one thought much about the proofs, especially the Post Office Department and Bureau of Engraving and Printing. Postmaster General Farley related in his autobiography, *Behind the Ballots*, that the genesis of presenting die proofs of stamps went back to the years 1903 to 1905. At that time the Post Office Department compiled a list of stamp gifts that comprised 140 U.S. die proofs from the first stamp issued in 1847 to the stamps of 1902, richly bound in albums and presented to 73 notable Republican statesmen.

These included President Theodore Roosevelt, Senator Henry Cabot Lodge of Massachusetts, G.O.P. Speaker of the House Joseph Cannon, and other senators, congressmen and members of the Cabinet.

Farley further related that "on various dates between 1923 and 1929, a total of 470 die proofs were given to successive incumbents who acted as Postmaster General and forty die proofs were given to the late President Coolidge who was then in office. Mrs. Warren G. Harding received one set of die proofs and Mrs. Coolidge received three . . . The foregoing recital is only a very meager record of the bighearted way in which souvenir stamps were passed out to the faithful during the long years when Republican worthies sat in authority.

". . . The question naturally arises, why did I neglect or overlook publication of these facts during the time when the souvenir stamps distributed by me were under fire? The reason why the records were not revealed then was closely tied up with my own notion of how a public official should act under criticism and, wisely or unwisely, I followed the only course of conduct which seemed fair under the circumstances. In the first place I had done nothing unethical and nothing that was to cost the government money, and therefore it was against my policy to apologize, to beg off, or to seek refuge behind any kind of excuse. The simple record of the transaction was made public and that was enough. In the second place, it has always seemed to me that the weakest kind of defense is to point to another person and say, 'He did it too.' "[5]

George Sloane, who had appraised the FDR collection at $80,000, estimated that the die proofs alone were worth approximately $40,000. Stamp collectors, philatelic writers and many citizens at large were aghast that the die proofs presented to the president would be included in the stamp auction that would benefit his estate. Many were of the opinion that the die proofs were the property of the U.S. government and should have been returned to the government after Roosevelt's death.

Stamp collector J. Cline McKenna was quoted in *The New York Times* as saying that the executors of Roosevelt's estate were "making a racket out of a hobby." McKenna contended that the die proofs were given to FDR with the understanding that they would be put on exhibition if the stamp collection was ever broken up. "There is plenty of time to conduct an investigation of the justification of putting these proofs up for auction with the rest of the collection. I do not believe they were given to Mr. Roosevelt with the idea of furthering his own estate."[6]

Other collectors contended that the auctioning of the die proofs went "against the ethics of the philatelic fraternity." To many it was merely another example of the scandal that started with the Farley stamps in which FDR and others were given sheets of stamps that were imperforate and ungummed, taken from the presses of the BEP. When the public protested against officials being presented with these stamp varieties, the Post Office Department was forced to produce the same varieti!es for collectors. Feelings were high at that time that no one would know the true extent of stamp gifts to political officials. FDR's die proofs were to them just one more piece of evidence of the clandestine stamp activities that went on in the Post Office Department.

"It is true," said Philatelic Society of Pittsburgh president James Sprague, "that the auction will make many more stamps available to the public, but those die proofs were given to Mr. Roosevelt as an official of the Government. They belong to the Government and should be part of the archives."[7]

Hobbies magazine, in its January 1946 issue, informed its readers that "the Roosevelt stamp collection is about to be sold at auction. "The magazine reported, "Some of those stamps were issued illegally, and the buyers ought to be warned that some day they will be seized . . . In talking to the best lawyer philatelist we know, he remarked that if the stamps had been left to the public in a museum, there probably would have been no sentiment to prosecute, because there would have been no evidence of intentional wrong doing. 'However,' he said, 'when such issues are sold for the benefit of the family, there will no doubt some day be a prosecution in the case.' " The editorial also stated that "the President is not above the law, and . . . he, of all people, should strictly obey the laws of the country and not assume the attitude that 'the king can do no wrong.' "[8]

Congress was deluged with letters from the public demanding a stop to the sale of the die proofs and an investigation into the legal ownership of the proofs. They questioned not only FDR's right to have owned them, but the right of successful bidders at auction to retain them after purchase. The Post Office Department and the Department of Justice rendered their opinion that it was perfectly legal to buy, sell and own die proofs of U.S. stamps.

While many philatelic writers wrote articles that made it seem that the auctioning of die proofs was something new, George Sloane, writing in the January 19 issue of *Stamps*, pointed out that die proofs that were part of the collections of other noted government officials from the Theodore Roosevelt, Warren Harding and Calvin Coolidge administrations regularly came up for sale at public auctions. *The New York Times* reported, "United States die proofs long have been bought and sold freely in the public market. Scott's specialized catalogue of United States stamps chronicles and prices about 300 varieties of such proofs run off from 1847 to date by private bank note companies and the Bureau of Engraving and Printing. Published records show that no protest against sale of them was made prior to the present controversy regarding the proofs in the Roosevelt estate."[9]

Linn's Stamp News agreed that precedents for the gift die proofs had been set years before. The publication had no quarrel with the auctioning of these proofs. The newspaper was adamantly opposed to the inclusion of "what is stated to be progressive die proofs of certain stamps, proofs of partially finished dies and the like. Material which under no circumstances ever should be left out of the Bureau.

"The suggestion is made by some correspondents and in some clippings that an injunction should be gotten out against the sale of this part of the collection and that it should be returned to the Bureau or placed in the Hyde park museum. We can heartily agree with this suggestion, but who is there to ask for such an injunction?

"Might we suggest that this would be a splendid place for the American Stamp Dealers Association to put in its ear in the interest of clean Philately. The American Philatelic Society or the Society of Philatelic Americans or even the Collectors Club of New York might take this step or one or more of the mentioned organizations might act jointly.

"Here is an opportunity for organized Philately to show its strength and doubtless an injunction could readily be had if proper steps were taken.

"Let this business be stopped now. How do we know that when the Ickes collection, which also flourished during the Farley regime, comes on the market, that we will not be faced with a situation similar to this one."[10]

Since the Post Office Department and Justice Department had rendered their opinion on the die proofs, FDR's executors stated on January 15, 1946, that the die proofs would be sold as scheduled on February 4.

FDR Stamp Auction First Session
February 4, 1946, 8 p.m.

As the auction of the Franklin Delano Roosevelt stamp collection opened at 8 p.m. on Monday, February 4, 1946, the first items up for sale were the controversial die proofs, which were divided into 139 lots along with another lot that offered the four albums and fleece-lined dust cases that housed the proofs.

The first lot offered was the complete set of 13 large-size normal-color die proofs for the 1894 set of regular stamps in 1¢ to $5 denominations (Scott 246-63). The auction catalog estimated the value of the set at $165, but bidding soon left catalog values in the dust, setting a trend that would continue throughout the auction. The set was finally gaveled down at $800.

There quickly followed proofs for the 1898 Trans-Mississippi series (Scott 285-93), catalog $180, and the 1901 Pan-American series (Scott 294-99), catalog $90. The sets brought $500 and $200 respectively.

The first 41 lots in the sale represented die proofs up to the 1929 George Rogers Clark commemorative (Scott 651) and brought $16,690 for the estate.

Lots 42 through 64 came up next and were described as "commemorative proofs die sunk on India paper on large cards, are heretofore known only on wove paper." The proofs began with the 1929 Edison commemorative (Scott 654) and continued on to the 1933 Century of Progress 1¢ and 3¢ issues (Scott 728-29). Each lot was termed "only one known," and the 22 lots sold for a total of $6,045.

Next up were three lots featuring the 1933 3¢ Newburgh commemorative (Scott 727), and the 1¢ and 3¢ Century of Progress issues. The catalog described the lots as the "MOST IMPORTANT GROUP OF ESSAYS & PROOFS IN STATES OF PRODUCTION." Each lot consisted of five die proofs of each stamp in various degrees of production from the first frame outline to the complete final proof. The Newburgh proofs (lot 65) sold for $1,050, while the 1¢ Century of Progress (lot 66) and the 3¢ Century of Progress proofs (lot 67) sold for $1,100 and $1,200, respectively, adding $3,350 to the estate.

There next followed 11 lots of large die proofs of U.S. airmail issues, beginning with the first U.S. airmail stamp issued in 1918 (Scott C1) and continuing through the 1932 8¢ Winged Globe issue (Scott C17). Lots 68, 69 and 70, featuring the first three U.S. airmail stamps, were first offered for bids individually and then offered as a complete set (lot 71). The auction catalog stipulated that "if the bid on the set exceeds the total bids on the three single lots they will be sold as a set." Individually, the proofs received bids for $700 (C1), $500 (C2) and $750 (C3), totaling $1,950. But as a set, the proofs brought in a bid of $2,800, for which they were finally sold. The rest of the airmail proofs (lots 72-8) brought an additional $5,600.

Special delivery, registration, postage due, postal savings mail, newspaper and special handling stamp proofs were offered next in lots 79 through 93, with lot 94 consisting of 11 matching albums in which the large die proofs were housed. These, the last of the large-size proofs, sold for a total of $5,995, and with 46 lots of small die proofs remaining, George Sloane's appraisal of $40,000 for all the die proofs had already been surpassed with a total of $40,480.

The small die proofs were offered in 46 lots and included U.S. commemoratives, beginning with the 1898 Trans-Mississippi set and concluding with the 1933 Newburgh commemorative. Also included were small proofs for the 1927 Lindbergh 10¢ airmail issue (Scott C10) and the 1930 Graf Zeppelin set (Scott C13-C15), as well as a lot of four matching binders and fleece-lined cases embossed with the president's name, the U.S. coat of arms and the legend "United States Commemorative Postage Stamp Issues of the Bureau of Engraving and Printing." These small die proofs, lots 95 through 140, provided an additional $13,170, bringing the grand total of die proof revenue to $53,650.

With the controversial die proofs now out of the way, the next order of business was the sale of 126 lots of autographed mint sheets of U.S. stamps, comprising the stamps issued during the Roosevelt administration except for one, a sheet of 1929 1½¢ Kansas overprints (Scott 659). Each of these sheets was autographed in the margins by Roosevelt, and most of them were also signed by Secretary of the Treasury Henry Morgenthau Jr. Other sheets were signed by various people, including Interior Secretary Harold Ickes, Postmaster General James A. Farley, Admiral Richard E. Byrd and other Cabinet members and politicos.

The mint sheets, sold as lots 141 through 266, realized the substantial amount of $26,845. The sheets of Newburgh Peace stamps (Scott 727) and the 1¢ and 3¢ Century of Progress issues (Scott 728-29) represented the first stamps issued during the Roosevelt administration, and were autographed by FDR and each member of his Cabinet. These sheets, lots 143, 145 and 147, were mounted on stout white cards, and each sold for $325.

Lots 267 through 291 were the final lots for the first day of the sale. These 25 lots comprised blocks and strips of imperforate original printings of stamps that were made at the time the perforated stamps were issued. These original imperforates consisted of the 1934 National Parks issues (Scott 740-49) and the 1934 American Philatelic Society and Trans-Mississippi souvenir sheets. Also represented were 10 covers of imperforate plate blocks addressed to FDR and signed by Secretary of the Interior Ickes. The covers sold for $525, and the entire selection of imperforates sold for $1,905. Figure 53 shows a set of imperforate National Parks singles.

Figure 53. FDR's set of National Parks imperforate singles.

The first session of the sale of the Roosevelt collection wrapped up with a total of $80,495 in sales. The first session alone surpassed the appraisal of the entire collection. Bidders seemed to be unconcerned with catalog values and estimates. In an effort to make something from the president's collection their own, especially something as interesting as die proofs and autographed sheets, people were more than willing to pay top dollar.

First Sale, Second Session

The second session of the first sale opened at 2 p.m. on the afternoon of Tuesday, February 5, 1946. The first items auctioned were eight lots of uncut sheets of original printings comprising the first stamp issues of the Roosevelt administration, the 3¢ Newburgh (Scott 727), Byrd Antarctic issue (Scott 733), 1934 Mother's Day (Scott 738), Wisconsin Tercentenary (Scott 739), National Parks series (Scott 740-49), APS and Trans-Mississippi souvenir sheets (Scott 750-51) and the 1934 16¢ special delivery airmail stamp (Scott CE1). These nine lots mostly comprised full uncut sheets of four panes, each numbering from 100 to 400 stamps, which were presented to FDR by Farley as they were produced at the Bureau of Engraving and Printing. The sheets are dated and autographed by Farley, who inscribed each, stating that they were the first sheet of each stamp produced and purchased for FDR's collection. The nine lots brought $4,425.

The president's U.S. collection was next offered in 213 lots, made up of regular U.S. postage and commemoratives (lots 307-73); FDR's first-day cover collection (lots 374-404, an example is shown in Figure 54); battleship covers (lots 405-11); airmail issues (lots 412-35); occupation mail (lots 436-37); Official stamps (lots 438-41); envelopes (lots 442-45); revenues (lots 446-47); encased postage (lot 449); locals (lots 450-51); telegraph-stamps presentation album (lot 452); Christmas seal presentation album (lot 453); miscellaneous U.S.

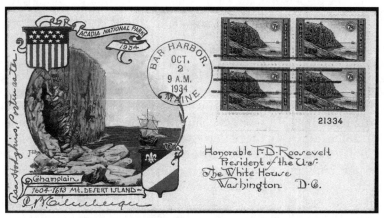

Figure 54. FDR's first-day cover of the 7¢ National Parks issue.

stamps in envelopes, including many duplicates (lots 454-66); Confederate States issues (lots 467-70); and U.S. possessions comprising stamps from the Canal Zone, Cuba, Guam, Hawaii, Philippines and Puerto Rico (lots 471-520).

Among the many interesting items in these lots was an 1884 letter written and signed by former President Ulysses S. Grant (lot 462) and a solo-flight cover addressed to FDR and signed by Amelia Earhart on January 11, 1935 (lot 426). Lot 404 was made up of 52 envelopes FDR described as his "bouquets and brickbats," which, as discussed earlier, were envelopes addressed to the president in complimentary or derogatory fashion.

These 213 lots of U.S. items brought $27,930. The bouquets and brickbats collection was sold to Gimbels Department Store in New York City for $525. The telegraph-stamps collection (lot 452) also sold for $525, while the Christmas seals presentation collection (lot 453) sold for $900.

The final items in the second session of the sale consisted of 92 lots representing presentation albums and collections given to the president by foreign leaders and dignitaries of Latin American nations. The first 73 lots comprised items from a collection given to FDR by Argentine collectors on the occasion of his visit to Buenos Aires in 1936 (lots 521-93). These lots sold for $2,440. They were followed by presentation collections from Brazil, Costa Rica, Cuba, Haiti, Mexico, Panama and two presentation booklets from Paraguay (lots 594-613), which sold for a total of $4,950.

The Costa Rican collection (lot 595) was a gold-medal-winning exhibition collection compring 967 stamps issued from 1862 through 1939. The collection was formed by Alfredo Moya of San Jose, Costa Rica, who won medals for it at the 1932 First Philatelic Exhibition in Costa Rica and the 1938 First Central America Philatelic Exhibition held in Guatemala. Both medals were included with the collection, which was presented to Franklin Roosevelt by the Costa Rican minister in 1940. This collection sold for $3,250. Revenue from the 92 lots of presentation collections was $7,390.

With the dispersal of the Latin American presentation albums, the second session of the Roosevelt sale closed.

First Sale, 3rd and Final Session

The final session of the first sale of the Roosevelt collection opened on Tuesday evening, February 5, 1946, at 8 p.m. and consisted of the president's general collection of stamps of the Latin American nations in 270 lots numbered 614 through 885. These lots comprised collections from Argentina (lots 614-33); Bolivia (lot 634); Brazil (lots 635-48); Central America (lot 649); Chile (lots 650-51); Colombia (lots 652-58); Costa Rica (lots 659-67); Cuba (lots 668-69); Dominican Republic (670-724, which included many die proofs and essays); Ecuador (lots 725-42); Guatemala (lots 743-46); Haiti (lots 747-83); Honduras (lots 784-85); Mexico (lots 786-88); Nicaragua (lots 789-92); Panama (lots 793-805); Paraguay (lots 806-7); Peru (lots 808-14); Philippines (lot 815); Sal-

Figure 55. This set of overprinted Ecuador stamps, from FDR's collection, commemorates Vice President Henry Wallace's visit to that country.

vador (lots 816-19); Uruguay (lots 820-73); and Venezuela (lots 874-77). The final eight lots, 878 through 885, consisted of a selection of albums and binders used to house these collections. A set of three Ecuador stamps commemorating a visit by Vice President Henry Wallace is shown in Figure 55.

Since Latin American stamps were some of the favorite and earliest stamps collected by FDR, many nations like Haiti and the Dominican Republic were represented by nearly complete collections. The final 270 lots of Latin American stamps brought a total of nearly $12,000.

As the first sale of the Roosevelt collection came to an end, only about half of the cataloged stamps that made up the president's collection had been sold. Nevertheless, nearly $135,000 had already been realized from the first 885 lots, far surpassing the $80,000 appraisal that had been made prior to the sale.

H.R. Harmer, shown in Figure 56, estimated that nearly 800 collectors attended the first three sessions of the Roosevelt auction, and that they purchased nearly every lot above market prices. Harmer also announced that part 2 of the Franklin Roosevelt sale would take place in three sessions, beginning Monday, April 1, 1946, at 8 p.m. and wrapping up with two sessions on Tuesday, April 2, 1946, at 2 p.m. and 8

Figure 56. H.R. Harmer, head of the firm that auctioned the FDR collection.

p.m. Public viewing of the stamps would be held from March 27 to April 1.

In late February, Harmers received a letter dated February 20, 1946, from the executors of the president's estate, complimenting them on a job well done:

> "Dear Mr. Harmer,
>
> "We extend our heartiest congratulations on the successful completion of the sale of the first portion of the stamp collection of the late President Roosevelt. The fine result accomplished by you speaks more strongly than anything we can say.
>
> "The record attendance for the opening session of the auction and widespread interest shown in the sale are a tribute to the efficient manner in which you handled the collection from the time it was turned over to you. We believe that the foresight and understanding displayed by you, not only with the advertising, preparation and publication of the catalogue, but also in the exhibition and conduct of the auction, left nothing to be desired.
>
> "We leave the sale of the second part of the collection on April 1st and 2nd in your hands with the fullest confidence."

Roosevelt Auction, Part Two

The first session of part two of the Roosevelt auction took place at the Parke-Bernet galleries at 8 p.m. on Monday, April 1, 1946. With Bernard Harmer and A.N. Bade conducting the sale, the session opened with an extensive specialized collection of Venezuelan stamps prepared by the Philatelic Society of Venezuela and presented to FDR in 1944. The collection was offered in 106 lots, which comprised a complete collection of Venezuelan stamps in singles, as well as blocks of stamps. Many of the stamps were featured as color, perforation and overprint varieties, both cataloged and uncataloged, and a host of color and printing errors.

Some of the more interesting items consisted of sets of airmail stamps in imperforate blocks of four, sets of provisional stamps with inverted surcharges, blocks of airmail stamps with double impressions, and a collection of regular stamps from 1893-1900 including various uncataloged reprints. The Venezuelan lots brought a total of $7,974.

The next eight lots, 107-14, represented a nearly complete collection of Belgian stamps up to and including German occupation issues of World War II. Also offered were imperforate reprints of six early issues and three early stamps overprinted "SPECIMEN." This presentation collection was inscribed to Roosevelt by the director general of the Belgium Postal Administration and dated on inauguration day, January 20, 1945. These eight lots were sold for a total of $1,194.50.

Lot 115 comprised a small presentation book containing a complete set of small die proofs of the 1911 pictorials from Bulgaria in their original colors. The 80mm by 130mm book contained, opposite the dedication page, the president's signature dated 1942 and the notation in the president's hand: "From George Earle, Minister to Bulgaria. This is said to be the only set in existence." The presentation book sold for $650.

The next presentation collection consisted of a nearly complete collection of the stamps of China from 1878 to 1941. The collection was presented to FDR by Generalissimo Chiang Kai-shek and included stamps that were produced but never issued. These stamps were considered to be "of the greatest rarity" and probably the "only ones in philatelic hands."

Broken down into lots 116-77, the Chinese collection was first bid on as individual lots and then was opened to be sold as an entire collection. The collection was mounted in a green silk-covered album with a gold inscription and slipcase. It comprised a dedication page handwritten in Chinese, three printed pages listing contents and 64 pages of stamps. Harmers described it as "A MAGNIFICENT AND PROBABLY UNIQUE COLLECTION OF GREAT VALUE." As lot 178, the Chinese presentation collection sold as a complete collection at $4,700.

Three smaller presentation collections of Chinese stamps were offered as lots 179-81 and brought $390.

Lot 182 offered a presentation collection of souvenir sheets from Czechoslovakia mounted in a loose-leaf album inscribed in the president's hand "Franklin D. Roosevelt, The White House, 1939." This lot sold for $275.

There followed presentation collections of Danish West Indies stamps from 1866 through 1917 (lot 183); 10 lots of stamps from Denmark presented to FDR by the director of the Danish Post Office, C.T. Mondrup (lots 184-93); and Dutch Indies stamps and covers from 1941-42 (lot 194). A total of $520 was garnered for these lots.

A presentation collection from the Ministry of Posts, Telegraphs and Telephones of France was next on the agenda. The first 25 lots (195-219) consisted of die proofs of select stamps from 1927 through 1939. These "Proofs de Luxe," individually mounted on blank album pages, were approximately 6 inches by 5 inches in original colors and bore the inscription "Atelier de Fabrication des Timbres-Poste: Paris" in the lower-right-hand corner. The balance of the French presentation collection consisted of four lots (220-23), including a sheet of the 1939 Red Cross stamp, a collection of stamps from French Andorra and a red bound stamp album and case containing the president's signature and the notation, "A personal present from a friend among the Free French in London." The 25 lots of die proofs sold for $1,740, while the remaining four lots sold for $1,115.

There followed four lots of presentation stamps and albums from Germany (lots 224-27); a collection of stamps issued by the German and Italian authorities in Greece 1941-44 (lot 228); a presentation stock book of 70 stamps from Italy 1930-35 (lot 229); a presentation leather booklet from the director

Figure 57. A collection of Norwegian stamps presented to FDR by Prince Olav in 1939.

general of Post and Telegraph of Mexico (lot 230); two lots of stamps from Monaco in a leather stock book (lot 231-32); a presentation folder containing 24 commemorative and semipostal stamps from the Netherlands 1934-38 (lot 233); and a presentation collection of 180 mint stamps of Norway 1905-39, mounted and annotated in a red leather binder signed by both FDR and Prince Olav of Norway at FDR's Hyde Park, New York, home on April 30, 1939. This collection was presented to FDR by the Philatelic Society of Oslo. The binder is shown in Figure 57.

The final 21 lots of presentation albums represented collections presented to the president from Poland (lots 235-36); a 1938 collection of stamps of the Portuguese colonies (lot 237); nine lots of stamps from the Soviet Union, including a presentation album of 848 stamps from 1921-34 mounted in an embossed loose-leaf album and signed by FDR and Soviet Ambassador Maxim Litvinov, April 10, 1934 (lots 238-46); a presentation collection of Swedish stamps 1855-1936 mounted in a blue album and signed by FDR with the notation, "The White House 1938, given me by the Swedish Director General of Posts," and a souvenir booklet with 74 stamps prepared for the Universal Postal Union Congress of 1939 (lots 247-48); a souvenir booklet of semipostal stamps of Switzerland presented to FDR by the Swiss director of Post, Telegraph and Telephone (lot 249); six lots of stamps in presentation folders from the Vatican (lots 250-54); and a booklet titled *Art and Postage Stamps* by Sheldon Cheney, which advocates more artistic designs for U.S. postage stamps (lot 255).

Lots 224 through 255 accounted for an additional $8,129. Bidding was high, as in the case of the presentation collection of 848 stamps from the Soviet Union (lot 242), which Harmer estimated at $700-plus in the catalog and which sold for $2,100.

The liquidation of the presentation collections ended the first session of part two of the Roosevelt collection.

Part Two, Second Session

The second session of the second sale opened at the Parke-Bernet Galleries on Tuesday, April 2, 1946, at 2 p.m. This session featured the president's general collection of worldwide stamps in 180 lots.

These lots comprised the president's collections from Abyssinia (lots 256-57); Afghanistan (lot 258); Algeria (259); Austria (260-62); Belgian East Africa (263); Belgium (264-66); Bulgaria (267); Camcroons (268-78); China (279-84); Congo (285-88); Curacao (289-94); Czechoslovakia (293); Danish West Indies (296-300); Denmark (301); Dutch Indies (302); Finland (303); France (304-10); French Colonies (311-14); French Equatorial Africa (315); French Oceania (316); Germany (317-26); German States (327-28); Greece (329); Greenland (330); Guadeloupe (331); Hungary (332); Iceland (333-36); Italy (337-39); Japan (340-42); Latvia (349-51); Lebanon (352-62); Liberia (363-64); Liechtenstein (365); Luxembourg (366-69); Manchukuo (370); Martinique (371); Monaco (372); Nejd (373-75); Netherlands (376-80); Norway (381-82); Obock (383-84); Persia (385); Philippines (386); Poland (387-88); Romania (389); Roman States (390-93); Russia (394-401); Saar (402-4); St. Marie de Madagascar (405); St. Pierre and Miquelon (406); Senegal (407); Siam (408-9); Somali Coast (410); Spain (411); Surinam (412); Sweden (413-15); Switzerland (416-21); Syria (422); Tibet (423-26); Tripolitania (427); Turkey (428-36); and Yugoslavia (343-48).

These lots comprised collections of stamps mounted on album pages and in stock books, many with handwritten notations by the president, as well as full sheets of stamps, blocks, covers and die proofs. They represented the many miscellaneous collections of stamps that FDR mounted and annotated. These 180 lots brought an additional $20,537 to the estate.

Next up was the president's collection of the British Empire, represented first by 39 lots of presentation collections. The first lot consisted of a folder of stamps from Australia (437). Next were four lots from Canada comprising large die proofs of regular and airmail stamps issued in 1942-43 to publicize Canada's contribution to the war effort (lots 438-41).

A superb collection of stampless covers from the Cape of Good Hope was next presented in 31 lots. These covers made up a nearly complete collection of all the postal markings in use from 1792-1853. The collection was presented to FDR by A.A. Jurgens of Cape Town (lots 442-72).

There followed a collection of 19 cards from Sir Alan Cobham to his wife, which he mailed to her from places along the route he took on his trailblazing flight from London to Cape Town — November 16, 1925, to February 17, 1926 — mounted in a loose-leaf album (lot 473); a presentation collection in a leather album from the Irish Free State signed by the president (lot 474); and a leather stock book of New Zealand health stamps issued from 1929-44 (lot 475). These presentation collections netted $5,010.

The final items in the second session were the stamps that made up the president's general collection of the British Empire. Lots were offered from FDR's collections from Antigua (lots 476-78); Australia (479); Bahamas (480-

88); Barbados (489-92); Bermuda (493-501); British Guiana (502-3); British Honduras (504-6); Canada (507-14); Cape of Good Hope (515-18); Cayman Islands (519-21); Ceylon (522); Cyprus (523-24); Dominica (525-29); Egypt (530); Gambia (531); Gibraltar (532); Gilbert and Ellice Islands (533); Gold Coast (534); Great Britain (535-50); and Grenada (551-54).

These lots were made up of single stamps, sets, blocks, sheets, covers, color errors and, in the case of lot 535 from Great Britain, nine original sketches by artist George Cruikshank along with a two-page letter addressed to him and dated February 2, 1840, with postmark, wax seal and the words "Favored by Rowland Hill" upon it.

An additional $4,020 was generated from the British Empire collections. Bidding exceeded catalog estimates in most cases. The lot (531) of 13 covers bearing 1938-44 pictorials from Gambia, for example, had an estimated value of $12.05-plus, but sold for $42.50. Likewise, Great Britain lot 539, which featured a single 2½ penny 1935 Silver Jubilee Prussian Blue color error, was estimated at $175 but was gaveled down at $350.

Thus did the second session of the Roosevelt sale part two come to an end, with the third session scheduled for the next evening at 8 p.m.

Part Two, Third Session

The third session of part two of the Roosevelt auction took place on Tuesday evening, April 2, 1946, at 8 p.m. As scheduled, this session was originally to have signaled the end of the auction of the Roosevelt collection. Harmer auctioneers had saved the president's favorite collection for last: the stamps of Hong Kong, the collection started by his grandfather for his mother and passed down to FDR when he was age 10.

Also scheduled for this final session was a group of miscellaneous stamps from around the world, a group of binders and albums from FDR's many collections, and a selection of philatelic literature ranging from Scott catalogs to specialized handbooks for the stamps of Hong Kong and Egypt.

The session opened with 180 lots of the stamps of Hong Kong. The auction catalog called attention to the fact that Hong Kong was FDR's favorite country. Since FDR had maintained this collection from childhood and had added every stamp and cover that had come his way, Harmer noted that there were many defective items in the collection that had not been included in the stated estimates.

Many of the stamps in these lots were sold as sets mounted on the original album pages. "The album pages," Harmer noted, "have, in most cases, been written up in the President's handwriting; many interesting varieties of shade and cancellation are included in the majority of the lots."

Many of the Hong Kong lots consisted of covers ranging from a stampless cover dated July 21, 1845, to covers bearing various denominations from Hong Kong's first stamp set in 1862 and subsequent sets.

The Hong Kong collection was full of rare stamps, covers and postmarks.

Lot 589 consisted of an unlisted imperforate block of 30¢ stamps (Scott 19) with an inscribed margin. Several lots contained stamps featuring inverted watermarks, and others included stamps with scarce postmarks.

On the other hand, the collection was also filled with what today would be termed seconds — stamps with small faults, tears, creases, heavy cancels and the like. These things did not bother FDR. He collected stamps for pure enjoyment and not for monetary gain. Many of the seconds represented a stamp with a slight vignette shift, double impression or slight shade variety. These were things that interested FDR and prompted him to include these stamps in his collection.

The stamps and covers of Hong Kong were offered in 80 lots (555-634) and sold for $4,465.

Next up were 69 lots of miscellaneous British Empire country collections. These consisted of collections from India (lot 635-37); Irish Free State (638-39); Jamaica (another of FDR's favorite countries, lots 640-46); Kenya and Uganda (647); Leeward Islands (648-54); Malta (655); Montserrat (656-57); Newfoundland (658-68); New Guinea (669); New Zealand (670-72); Nova Scotia (673); Papua (674); Queensland (675); St. Christopher (676); St. Kitts-Nevis (677-79); St. Lucia (680-85); St. Vincent (686-88); Southern Rhodesia (689); Straits Settlements (690); Trinidad (691-92); Trinidad and Tobago (693-97); Turks and Caicos Islands (698); Union of South Africa (699-700); and the Virgin Islands (701-3). Pages of St. Kitts-Nevis blocks from the Roosevelt collection are shown in Figure 58. These British Empire collections sold for $4,407.

Thirty-six lots of miscellaneous worldwide stamp sets followed next. These miscellaneous lots featured stamps, souvenir sheets and covers from many British colonies as well as a host of European nations. Most were mounted on album pages and made up complete collections. Also represented was a large box filled with several thousand stamps sorted into envelopes by country (lot 731). Offered as lots 738-39 were German propaganda, including an underground newspaper and sheet of labels featuring Hitler and skull and crossbones, which were produced in Switzerland and mailed to the next of kin of German casualties. Lot 740 consisted of 188 match-box cover labels in a loose-leaf album, which was presented to FDR and was inscribed by FDR in the flyleaf: "Franklin D. Roosevelt. A very interesting collection."

These final lots of stamps sold for a total of $7,510. The large box of stamps sorted into envelopes by country (lot 731) sold for $550. The propaganda newspaper (lot 738) brought $360. The sheet of Hitler labels produced in Switzerland was purchased for $1,300, and the collection of match-box cover labels sold for $150.

Eighteen lots consisting of album binders used to house many of the FDR collections were offered next. Many of these binders and albums were expensively produced pieces. Most were produced exclusively for the president and were typically imprinted with the name of the country on the cover and spine, as well as embossed with the president's name and/or the presi-

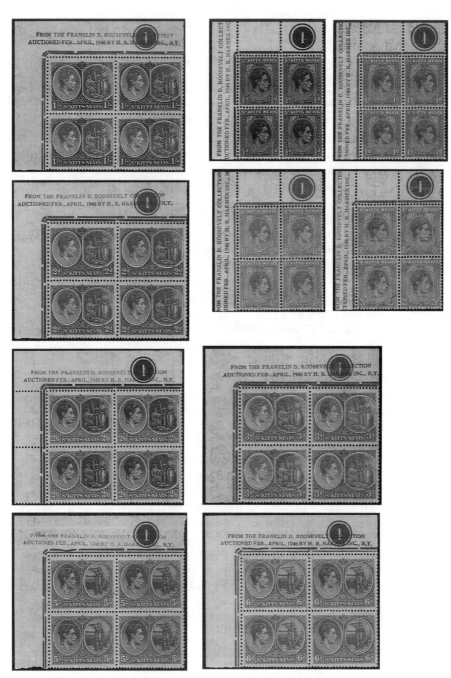

Figure 58. St. Kitts-Nevis blocks from the Roosevelt collection.

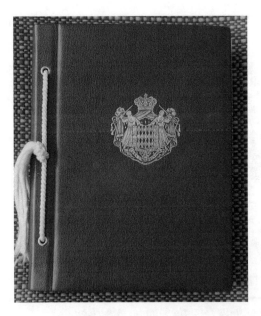

Figure 59. This album binder housed FDR's Monaco stamp collection.

dential seal of the United States. An album binder that housed a collection of Monaco stamps is shown in Figure 59.

These lots (741-58) brought an additional $2,010, and most bidders were happy to pay high prices to get an FDR embossed album. A lot consisting of eight black spring-back binders imprinted with the names of British colonies and embossed "F.D.R." sold for $160 (lot 745), while a single album (lot 757), described in the catalog as a "beautiful loose-leaf blank album, size 10x11½ ins. with 200 pages and interleaves, dark blue and gold bordered binder with imprint Franklin D. Roosevelt," was purchased for $490.

The final 20 lots of the session consisted of philatelic literature and featured a Scott 1942 *Specialized Catalogue of United States Stamps* with gilt-edged pages and imprinted FRANKLIN D. ROOSEVELT in gold on the cover, which was initialed and dated by the president (lot 759). Also represented, among others, were the *Specialized Catalogue of Canadian Airmail Stamps, Air Post Stamps of Colombia, The Stamps of the Danish West Indies, Postage and Telegraph Stamps of Peru* and *Catalogue of the Tuberculosis Seals of the World*.

A single lot was offered featuring the January-through-June editions of *Gibbons Stamp Weekly* from 1910 and a full edition of *The London Philatelist* from 1912 (lot 776). Lot 777 offered a box of miscellaneous pamphlets, price lists, periodicals and auction catalogs including plates from the famous Arthur Hind collection of 1933.

The final lot (778) was described as "accessories: 17 linen covered boxes, 3 diff. sizes with hinged tops, 2 pocket size imitation leather bound stock books, linen strips; all used, fine condition."

Again, bidding was brisk. Not surprisingly, the 20 lots sold for $1,567. The highest realization was for lot 761, a *Sanabria Air Post Catalogue 1941* deluxe edition with gold imprint FRANKLIN D. ROOSEVELT on front, initialed and dated by the president. The catalog sold for $425.

The lot of various pamphlets, price lists, periodicals and auction catalogs (777) was gaveled down at $45, while the final lot of accessories (778)

*Figure 60. This sheet of Bell stamps from the Famous Americans
series was signed by FDR and Secretary Morgenthau.*

was purchased for $85. FDR's last catalog, Scott 1945 *Standard Postage Stamp
Catalogue*, received shortly before his death and imprinted FRANKLIN D.
ROOSEVELT in gold, was purchased for $60.

Naturally the influence of sentiment for the president, as well as the
chance to own one of his catalogs, albums or collections, especially if it was
initialed, autographed or accompanied by notations in the president's hand,
account for the high bidding and overwhelming interest in what was to have
been the final phase of the Roosevelt auction. Figure 60 shows a sheet of the
Alexander Graham Bell stamp (Scott 893), signed in the margins by FDR and
Treasury Secretary Morgenthau.

As the auction closed, the final totals were $26,687.50 for the first ses-
sion, $29,567.50 for the second session and $19,959 for the third session. The
grand total for part two was $76,214, and the combined grand total for the
entire auction had now surpassed the $200,000 mark.

Franklin D. Roosevelt Auction, Part Three

As mentioned earlier, many boxes of stamps and covers still lay packed
and unsorted at the time of FDR's death. It seemed possible that these boxes
might be auctioned just as they were because they contained such a vast amount
of items to be sorted and cataloged. As the Harmer staff went through these
boxes, however, they concluded that some of the most interesting and desir-
able items were contained within them.

After considerable sorting and cataloging, the auction house decided to open a third sale featuring "the first and major portion of this part of the President's stamps" on Tuesday, July 16, 1946. The auction would take place beginning at 2 p.m. at the premises of H.R. Harmer, and viewing of the lots was scheduled for July 11, 12, 13 and 15, between 9:30 a.m. and 4:30 p.m. and on auction day from 9:30 a.m. until 1:30 p.m.

The third auction catalog opened with an introduction by the Harmer staff:

"We feel that a few words of explanation will be of interest as a foreward to this further auction of stamps from the 'President Roosevelt' collection.

"It was generally known that apart from the collection in albums, presentation collections and autographed sheets, which we had the privilege of selling by auction in February and April last, there remained a large number of envelopes and stamps on portions of official correspondence that had been packed away in large boxes awaiting time for the president to classify and incorporate in his collection.

"The contents of this sale represent the first and major portion of this part of the president's stamps. In addition are included some items that the executors have found since the date of our first auctions, and a small number of lots sold in the previous Roosevelt auctions, offered by order of the present owners.

"Owing to general pressure of work, this is the first opportunity that we have had of dealing with this mass of correspondence and in preparing this catalogue we have reached the conclusion that this may well be considered in many ways the most interesting material yet offered. Many of these covers have been personally addressed to Roosevelt from his many thousands of admirers with the sole desire that they would form a part of his stamp collection; many bear interesting signatures of Pilots, Postmasters, high ranking Offices of the Armed Forces with cancellations that link up with the particular item or cachet concerned. There are naturally hundreds of unique souvenirs included; the majority of the envelopes and cards are of very clean and attractive appearance, so that the fortunate purchasers will not only have souvenirs but also covers that will prove a very real addition to their collections.

". . . It will be generally appreciated that the value of many of the lots submitted is largely of philatelic interest combined with sentiment. As philatelic experts we cannot attempt to value sentiment, therefore we must leave bidders to use their own judgment in making bids.

"We have done our best to offer these stamps in a form that will not only give the average collector an opportunity to acquire some interesting items but also permit the trade to obtain some large and valuable lots. It is the wish of the executors that these items should be as widely distributed as possible; it is our desire to cooperate in all possible ways and therefore we will do our utmost to assist out of town bidders on the large lots, as we feel that these stamps should be circulated not only in the distant parts of the United States,

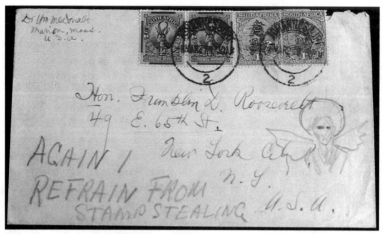

Figure 61. This cover from South Africa is addressed to FDR. A mailroom employee, evidently a stamp collector as well, added a drawing of an angel and the legend, "AGAIN I REFRAIN FROM STAMP STEALING."

but also in overseas countries as well."

The third auction of the collection of Franklin D. Roosevelt (International sale 16244, American sale 344) took place on the premises of H.R. Harmer Inc. on Tuesday, July 16, 1946, opening at 2 p.m. Interesting items, such as the cover shown in Figure 61, were auctioned in this session.

The first lots offered at the third sale consisted of anniversary, commemorative and assorted dedication covers the Harmer auction catalog described thus:

"Every item in this section comprising 196 lots is a letter or postcard personally addressed to Mr. Roosevelt, generally while he was President but in a few cases while he was Governor of New York, nearly every cover bears a distinctive cachet tying it up with the particular event, in a number of instances the envelopes bear signatures of important people connected with the Post Office or Services, also there are some hand drawn or printed cachets which are of very great interest. Every letter or card was a gift to the President for his collection. They are all clean and attractive and there are no duplicate covers in any lot."

The first 22 lots comprised covers addressed to the president from his many admirers. Lots included commemorative or anniversary covers in bundles numbering from five to 32 covers. These first lots sold for $575.50. Figures 62-64 show two such covers and a postal card.

Lots 23-45 were made up of hand-illustrated entires. Each cover bore a cachet that was hand-drawn and produced in either watercolor paints, pen and ink, pencil or bits of colored paper pasted to the envelopes. The last lot in this section, lot 45, was a cover addressed to "President Roosevelt Washington D.C." The address was formed by cut stamps pasted to the cover.

Figure 62. This 1934 cover commemorates the last delivery in flight of airmail by the Adams system to the Century of Progress exhibition in Chicago. The cover is signed by the Adams system inventor and the pilot.

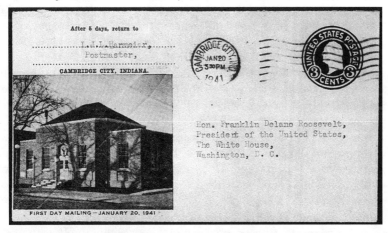

Figure 63. This inauguration cover postmarked January 20, 1941, was sent to President Roosevelt from Cambridge City, Indiana.

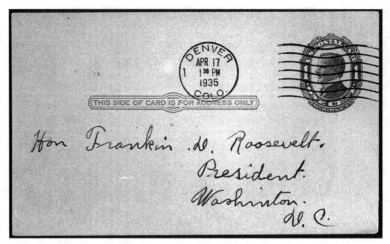

Figure 64. This postal card informed FDR that the sender supported the Townsend Plan more than FDR's plan for Social Security legislation.

The lots of hand-illustrated entires sold for $451.50. Lot 45 was purchased for $20.

Next up were 13 lots of Naval covers (lots 46-58). Each cover bore a Naval postmark, and several were autographed by admirals, captains and dignitaries at ship commissionings and other Naval events.

Several of these commemorated visits of the *USS Constitution* from January 1933 to April 1934. Each of these covers bore Naval postmarks to commemorate the visit of *Old Ironsides* to various Naval ports around the country.

Lot 47 was a single *USS Constitution* cover postmarked May 31, 1933, in Seattle, Washington, and autographed for President Roosevelt by Postmaster General Farley, the captain of the *Constitution* and the mayor of Seattle. Lot 52 was made up of 28 different *Constitution* covers, all with commemorative cachets and Naval postmarks. The lots of U.S. Naval covers brought $370.

Eight lots (59-66) were auctioned next. They consisted of entire covers addressed to FDR by means of a pictorial address. These interesting and innovative covers included such items as an entire addressed to FDR by means of 26 copies of the 1932 ½¢ George Washington issue (Scott 704) pasted to the cover in the shape of the letters "F.D.R." The cover (lot 62) is stamped "Insufficiently addressed" but reached the president nevertheless. Lot 63 was an entire commemorating the dedication of Lakeland Airport, sent to the president by three young sisters, ages 11, 13 and 14, and addressed to Roosevelt by pasted photos of FDR and the White House on the cover. These eight covers were gaveled down at $99.

Lots 67 through 74 consisted of oversize entires the Harmer catalog described as "some of the finest pieces from this portion of the President's Collection."

These eight lots contained such items as a 12-inch by 12-inch first-day cover franked with a complete set of the 1940 Famous Americans series (Scott 859-93) and canceled with a "Boston, Massachusetts, October 28, 1940, 9 a.m. first day of issue" postmark (lot 70); an 18-inch by 12-inch airmail entire bearing a plate number block of four of the 1938 6¢ airmail stamps (Scott C23) sent to FDR from San Diego, California, during National Airmail Week in 1938 and autographed by the designer of Charles Lindbergh's plane, the first superintendent of Air Mail Service and the postmaster of San Diego (lot 72); and a 21-inch by 14-inch card also bearing a plate number block of four of the 1938 6¢ airmail stamps. The card features a hand-drawn "New Bedford May 19, 1938" postmark, a hand-painted cachet and the signatures of all 168 employees of the New Bedford Post Office (lot 73). An oversize entire containing a stamp auction catalog from Cuba is shown in Figure 65. The eight lots of oversize entires sold for $240.50.

There followed five lots of new post office dedication covers (lots 75-79) and eight lots of assorted Roosevelt inauguration covers (lots 80-87). Lots 75-79 sold for $125, while the inauguration lots brought another $188.

In 1938, the United States celebrated National Airmail Week from May 15 through 21 to commemorate the first flights of the mails 20 years earlier. Post offices around the country participated in National Airmail Week by inaugurating many new airmail routes throughout the country and by applying cachets from their cities on covers being sent by airmail.

The Post Office Department released on May 14, 1938, a single 6¢ blue and carmine airmail stamp featuring an eagle, taken from a sketch made by President Roosevelt (Scott C23). It was hoped the new stamp would be used on covers for National Airmail Week and that the general public would participate.[11]

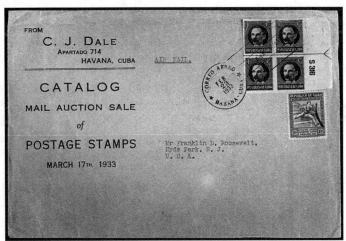

Figure 65. Even large envelopes containing Cuban auction catalogs found a place in FDR's collection.

Public participation greatly exceeded Post Office Department hopes. The event was such a huge success that President Roosevelt, Postmaster General James A. Farley and many members of the Post Office Department were inundated with thousands of covers from people all over the United States to add to their collections.

Farley estimated that mail from National Airmail Week alone accounted for an extra $1 million of revenue for his department.[12]

He received so many covers that he issued a press release on June 3, 1938, in which he thanked the country for their gifts:

> "I received such a deluge of air-mail greetings and cachet covers that for the first time in my life I am unable to write a personal acknowledgment to every sender. The greetings and covers sent me number many thousands. Other officials of the Post Office Department also received thousands of such greetings and covers and they, like me, find it impossible to reply to all of them. Therefore, we hope that all those who so kindly remembered us will accept this notice as evidence of our appreciation."[13]

Hundreds of National Airmail Week covers mailed to President Roosevelt by postmasters and admirers were the next items offered at the auction.

Twenty-two lots (88-109) of National Airmail Week covers, in bundles of from nine to 150 covers, were unveiled, all addressed to the president. All covers, except those in the last three lots, included a special city cachet from the city of origin, and many were first-flight covers as well.

As with all covers in this third portion of the Roosevelt auction, sentiment was the guide when it came to bidding. The Harmers catalog did not attempt to put a value on any of the covers in this sale, knowing full well from the previous two sales that sentiment would rule the day.

This certainly held true in regard to the National Airmail Week covers. The first and largest lot of 150 covers (lot 88) sold for $200, and the smallest lot of six covers (lot 106) was sold for $27.50. The amount garnered for all 22 lots totaled $1,822.

The next eight lots (110-17) consisted of a variety of covers commemorating events in the life of President George Washington. They sold for $292.50. There followed a single lot of 16 covers commemorating events in the life of President Abraham Lincoln (118), including covers commemorating the Lincoln Monument and the opening of the Lincoln Highway. Lot 118 sold for $27.50.

Lots 119 through 126 offered covers bearing postmarks from towns aptly named Franklin, Delano, Roosevelt, Democrat and President. Lot 119 consisted of three registered letters with appropriate fancy postmarks from Fox, Arkansas (a fox); Rattlesnake, Montana (a snake); and Flagstaff, Arizona (a flag). Lot 125 was a large envelope sent to the president from Santa Claus, Indiana, on Christmas 1932. The letter "R" of Roosevelt in the address was made up of 14 different stamps. These eight lots were sold for $130.

Autographed covers made up the next 12 lots (127-38) and featured a Spring Valley, New York, post office dedication cover postmarked April 3, 1937, and signed by Farley (lot 128); a 1944 3¢ Motion Pictures commemorative first-day cover (Scott 926) addressed to the president and autographed by actor Bela Lugosi (lot 131); and a cover (lot 138) commemorating the inauguration of Philatelic Broadcasts on January 8, 1938, and signed by Farley, Walter E. Koons of the National Broadcasting Company, H.L. Lindquist, Robert Graham and other distinguished collectors involved in the broadcast. The autographed covers realized $215.

A small section of three lots (lots 139-41) featuring covers bearing cachets for stamp exhibitions and societies sold for $38. These lots were followed by three lots of covers (142-44) commemorating the births of various U.S. presidents. The lots included a set of five covers postmarked on Roosevelt's 52nd birthday on January 30, 1934. A total of $37 was garnered from these covers.

Five single lots were offered next. Lot 145 offered 10 covers postmarked on various April 30 President's Day events ($15). Lot 146 was made up of three July 4 covers from 1933, 1934 and 1939 with stamped cachets ($15). Lot 147 comprised six Christmas greeting covers ($10). Lot 148 featured 10 different covers commemorating Mother's Day and other events ($15), and lot 149 showcased 10 covers with various dates, all franked with the 3¢ National Recovery stamp (Scott 732) and bearing printed, stamped or hand-drawn cachets ($20).

Three lots (150-52) featuring 17 1933 Century of Progress covers from the World's Fair in Chicago brought $70.50, followed by two lots (153-54) of 11 covers commemorating the *USS Akron,* realizing $30, and two lots (155-56) offering 12 1933 Beer covers celebrating the repeal of prohibition, which were purchased for $47.

The next 40 lots were made up of a variety of miscellaneous covers (lots 157-96), all addressed to the president and most bearing cachets. One common cover that found a home in FDR's collection is shown in Figure 66.

Among the items included in these lots were six covers bearing U.S. and Canadian stamps and commemorating the U.S.-Canada royal train trip by King George VI and Queen Elizabeth during June 1939 (lot 170); a $500 Confederate note sent to FDR by addressing the reverse and with the notation "Lost—but not forgotten" (lot 172); a 1933 Dick Merrill, New York-to-London-to-New York round-trip coronation flight cover bearing a note to FDR and signed by Merrill and his navigator John Lambie (lot 182); and an August 20, 1935, Los Angeles-to-New York stratosphere flight cover (lot 184) from pilot Wiley Post, bearing a plate block of six 16¢ special delivery airmail stamps of 1934 (Scott CE1) and postmarked Los Angeles on the front and Washington, D.C., on the reverse.

Also included were lots containing bundles of first-flight covers, Army

Figure 66. This airmail cover found a home in FDR's collection for two reasons: the misspelling of the name Franklyn and the 1¢ postage due.

Post Office cancels, patriotic cachets and dedication covers. The 40 lots were sold for $1,930.50.

The last section of covers consisted of 17 lots (197-213) of miscellaneous entires added to the president's collection but not addressed to him.

Most of the lots were made up of covers franked with Roosevelt-era stamps, and many were signed by Farley. A few interesting items were included in this section, among them in lot 198, a stampless cover postmarked April 20, 1838, and signed by FDR's great grandfather James, and a letter dated 1791 signed by FDR's great great grandfather Isaac Roosevelt. Lot 199 featured a stampless cover sent from the Indian Trade Office in Georgetown, D.C., to Major William McClennan.

The final lot (213) featured 12 1940 South Seas and South Pacific first-flight covers to and from Hawaii, Canton Island, New Zealand, New Caledonia and the United States. This last section of covers brought $716.50 for the Roosevelt estate. Three covers from this sale are shown in Figures 67-69.

Discovered in the several boxes of stamps making up this third sale were several fine U.S. stamps. These were offered in 36 lots.

The first 20 lots (214-33) included stamps from the 1893 Columbian series (Scott 230-45); a block of four 1½¢ Martha Washington stamps horizontally imperforate between from the 1938 Presidential set (Scott 805b); and a $5 1941 Defense postal savings stamp mounted in a savings book, with the notation in FDR's hand "First $5.00 Defense stamp sold at the Will Rogers Post Office, Clarence, Okla." (lot 230). These 20 lots sold for a total of $633.

Also discovered with these U.S. stamps was another small selection of autographed sheets of FDR-era stamps (lots 234-40) signed by the president and Treasury Secretary Henry Morgenthau Jr. Lot 241 featured the first sheet of the 5¢ United Nations stamp (Scott 928) sold at San Francisco on April 25, 1945. It was signed by the postmaster at San Francisco and purchased and signed by Secretary of State Edward Stettinius, who sent it along with a letter requesting that this last stamp approved by the president before his death on April 12, 1945, be added to his collection. This sheet sold for $60.

Also included in this section of U.S. stamps were lots made up of 18 assorted die proofs on cards (lot 243), 75 copies of 1862-71 2¢ U.S. Internal

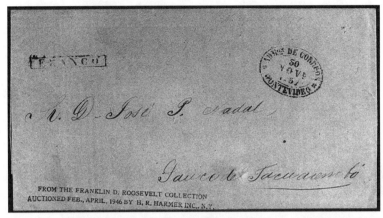

Figure 67. Stampless cover from Uruguay dated November 30, 1857.

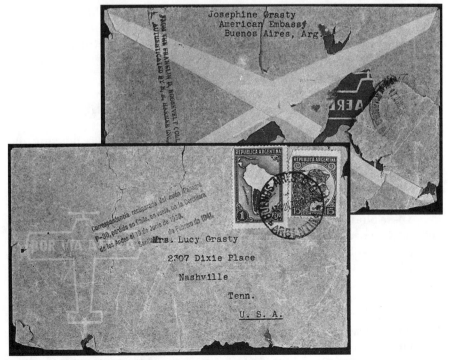

Figure 68. Crash cover from Arica, Chile, June 19, 1938.

Figure 69. An 1870s stamped envelope from Louisville, Kentucky.

Revenue stamps (Scott R15) in various-size blocks and affixed to documents (lot 244), three sheets of 1944 Pine Breeze Christmas labels showing progressive printing (lot 245) and three lots (247-49) of large envelopes containing hundreds of miscellaneous stamps. These final lots of U.S. stamps brought an additional $1,322.

Lot 250 was described in the Harmer catalog as a "Booklet entitled Art and Postage Stamps by Sheldon Cheney in which he advocates more artistic designs for our postage stamps, using as examples 23 European unused stamps partly stuck down in the booklet, also U.S. India paper proofs of the 5¢ 1875 reproduction issue and the 1863 2¢ black Jackson stamp listed at $21.50. This booklet is one of 93 copies done by the author at the Sleepy Hollow Press, Scarborough, 1923-26, and bears the President's notation 'FDR 1939' on the fly leaf." This booklet sold for $100.

Lots 251-54 were ring binders with fleece-lined cases housing the president's die-proof collections. Each binder was gold-embossed "United States Commemorative Postage Stamp Issues of the Bureau of Engraving and Printing," "Franklin Delano Roosevelt" and included the coat of arms of the United States.

These binders originally had been sold in the first auction as lot 140 for $400, but had been reoffered by order of the original purchaser. The four binders and cases sold for $200.

Nine lots of U.S. possessions made up of one lot of Canal Zone (lot 255), one of Hawaii (lot 256) and seven lots of Philippines (257-63) sold for a combined total of $266.50.

After disposing of the United States and possessions, next up that Tuesday afternoon were selections of general foreign stamps.

First auctioned were 28 lots of foreign airmail stamps and covers from Brazil (lots 264-66), Canada (267), Dominican Republic (268), Fiji (269), Germany (270), Haiti (271-72), Hungary (273), Liberia (274-75), Mexico (276-77), Nicaragua (278-79), Panama (280), Poland (281), Russia (282), Union of South Africa (283) and Venezuela (284-91). These lots sold for $1,144.

Next were 57 lots of general foreign regular postage issues from Antigua (lots 292-93), Argentina (294), Austria (295-96), Bahamas (297-98), Barbados (299), Belgium (300), Bermuda (301), Brazil (302), Cayman Islands (303), Cuba (304-5), Curacao (306), Czechoslovakia (307), Dominica (308), Dominican Republic (309-14), Dutch Indies (315), Germany (316-18), Great Britain (319), Greece (320), Haiti (321-22), Italy (323), Leeward Islands (327), Luxembourg (328), Newfoundland (329), Paraguay (330), Poland (330a-f), Roman States (331), Saar (332), Salvador (333), Tonga (334-35), Union of South Africa (336), Uruguay (337), Venezuela (338), Yugoslavia (324-26), British Colonies (339), British Colonies in America (340), Central and South America (341-42) and a general foreign lot of several hundred mixed stamps and covers (343).

Among the interesting items in this section of lots were an Argentina 1867-72 15¢ unwatermarked, imperforate stamp (Scott 16) with a British Philatelic Association certificate (lot 294) and Curacao cover addressed by the president to himself with an enclosed note by him stating, "Posted by me from U.S.S. Houston at St. Eustatiuson Feb. 1939" (lot 306). Greek Youth stamps (Scott 427-36, C38-47) used on three covers sent to FDR by Lincoln McVeagh, American minister to Greece, were included in lot 320. These stamps were good for postal duty for only three days. Lots 330a-f included Poland composite die essays for the 1921 Constitution commemorative (Scott 156-62) on glazed paper. These 57 lots garnered $1,770.50.

The three following lots consisted of various collections in binders.

Lot 344 featured four Scott Ne Plus Ultra binders, two Argentina and two Brazil with "F.D.R." imprinted in gold. Lot 345 featured two black springback binders housing FDR's Philippines and Dominican Republic Volume 3 collections, and three Scott Ne Plus Ultra binders stamped Uruguay 1, 2 and 3 respectively. All were imprinted "F.D.R." in gold. The last album lot (346) featured a single green, imitation-leather Bruce post binder with case. The three lots of binders sold for $110.

The next lots (347-73) consisted of American Consular Service correspondence. The Harmer catalog described them as "26 lots, all on portions of heavy Registered Mail, there are many large blocks and high value stamps included and though a small proportion are defective, the majority of the pieces are quite attractive. These have been sent from the American Consular Offices throughout the world and no U.S.A. stamps are included in this section."

The lots included collections of 200 large pieces on fronts of consular mail representing various countries, including Austria, Danzig, Greece and Switzerland (lots 347-51), as well as Consular Service items from British Empire nations (lots 352-58), Bahamas (359), Barbados (360-64), Bermuda (365), Burma (366-67), Danzig (368), French Colonies (369), Hong Kong (370-71) and Jamaica (372-73). These lots sold for a total of $670.50.

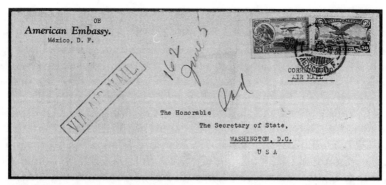

Figure 70. This American Embassy in Mexico cover was saved for the president by one of his children who wrote "Dad" on the cover.

Figure 71. A French cover from Roosevelt's collection.

Figure 72. This French cover is franked with a color error of the 1.50-franc SS Normandie stamp, Scott 300a.

Figure 70 shows an American Embassy in Mexico cover. One of FDR's children saved the cover for him, as witnessed by "Dad" printed on the front.

Boxes of stamps too numerous to sort through made up the last two sections and final 19 lots of this third sale. The first 11 lots (374-84) consisted of large boxes described as "practically full containing many hundreds of covers and some thousands of stamps, incl. high value blocks and a number of very interesting items; a lot well worth sorting, some of the covers are addressed to the President but the majority is from American Consulates abroad to the Secretary of State; mainly airmail covers and a very high proportion of air stamps is included." These boxes of stamps and covers sold for $2,970. Figures 71-73 show three French covers from FDR's collection, including one with a color error. Figure 74 shows a German cover addressed to the wrong President Roosevelt. Figure 75 shows a cover addressed to FDR from the Netherlands.

The final items of the third sale of the Roosevelt collection consisted of eight lots of various-size boxes "containing many thousands of stamps cut from correspondence, mainly registered mail including many blocks, Air Mail

Figure 73. The front and back of a French cover from Roosevelt's collection.

Figure 74. This German cover was erroneously addressed to "Theodore Roosevelt."

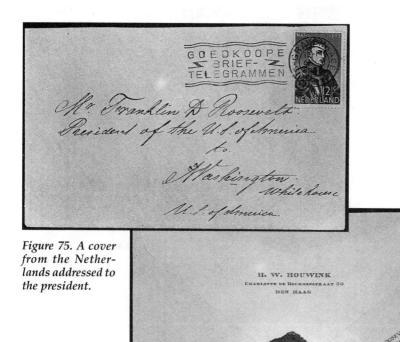

Figure 75. A cover from the Nether-lands addressed to the president.

stamps, British Colonials, South American, etc.; a good lot of considerable interest." These final eight lots were gaveled down at $540, bringing the third sale of the Franklin Roosevelt auction to an end.

It was no surprise that the bidding for the third sale was just as brisk as it had been for the previous two sales. Sentiment, however, played a major role in the third sale. The covers addressed to the president, and the sheets of stamps autographed by him, were for the most part ordinary stamps of the era. But to many, the opportunity to purchase items from the president's collection and to add them to their own collections was a once-in-a-lifetime opportunity.

Realizations for the third sale of Tuesday, July 16, 1946, resulted in a final total of $17,208.

The Franklin D. Roosevelt Auction, Part Four. First Session, Tuesday, December 17, 1946, 2 p.m.

The introduction to the catalog for the fourth sale began:

"In the introduction to the catalogue of part III of the Roosevelt collection, we explained in some detail the reason for holding over the large number of envelopes and stamps on portions of official correspondence that had been packed away in large cartons and which time did not permit us to include in the two main auctions on February 4/5 and April 1/2.

"When we originally glanced at the contents of these cartons we had no idea that they contained so many interesting items, or that we should find it necessary to devote three days of auctions to realize them.

"We present in this catalogue the last and final opportunity to purchase, from the original auctions, items from this world famous collection . . .

"At last we have completed describing and lotting the balance of the Roosevelt stamps and we feel that the result, as presented in this catalogue, has fully justified the time we have devoted to the task. Many of the lots are of a most attractive nature and we would particularly draw attention to the Air Mail week covers, the Consular Service correspondence and the cartons and boxes at the conclusion of the auction. Naturally some of the items are of philatelic interest combined with sentiment, but we feel that there are still many hundreds of collectors who wish to include in their albums a suitable memento of America's No. 1 Philatelist and we have done our best to offer a range of lots to please all types of bidders.

"We have not given 'estimated Cash Value,' as in a number of instances, sentiment forms a large part of the value. However we shall be happy to supply details of the approximate value of lots on request, these figures being largely based on our experience in the preceding Roosevelt auctions.

"And so, when the hammer falls on lot 542, we, at H.R. Harmer, Inc., will write 'Finis' to undoubtedly the most interesting, and at times, the most worrying experience of our careers, with the belief that the job has been well organized and well done. The executors echo our belief with the following comments recently received:

> 'I think you did excellent work in the way you handled the sale of the collection and deserve much commendation for its success.'
>
> Henry T. Hackett

> 'The fine job you did on this sale is further evidence that my faith in H.R. Harmer, Inc. was well placed.'
>
> Basil O'Connor

> 'I want to take this opportunity to tell you how excellently I think you handled this sale.'
>
> Eleanor Roosevelt"

The first session of the fourth auction, sale number 16270, American sale number 370, began at 2 p.m. Tuesday, December 17, 1946, and opened with U.S. covers.

"Unless otherwise stated," the catalog opened, "every item in this large section comprising lots 1-238 is a letter or postcard personally addressed to Mr. Roosevelt, generally while he was President, but in a few cases while he was Governor of New York, nearly every cover bears a distinctive cachet tying it up with the particular event, in a number of instances the envelopes bear signatures of important people connected with the Post Office or Services, also there are some hand drawn or painted cachets which are of very great interest. Every letter or card was a gift to the President for his collection. They are all clean and attractive and there are no duplicate covers in any lot unless otherwise stated."

The first 18 lots consisted of hand-illustrated entires and included such items as a January 30, 1939, cover bearing a watercolor painting of a March of Dimes motif for the president's 57th birthday (lot 2); a hand-painted third-term inauguration cover postmarked January 20, 1941 (lot 5); and an October 12, 1935, Stratford Hall, Virginia, dedication cover sent to the president by his mother Sara with the following note:

> "Dearest Franklin,
>
> "They tell me that this envelope will become available for a collection. There is great excitement here, and your message will be read. Weather is perfect. I am not getting up till noon.
>
> Thinking of you always,
Mama"

The lots of illustrated entires sold for $245.

Nine lots (19-27) of autographed covers were up next. All were signed or initialed by the president and featured an *SS Manhattan* first-voyage cover of August 10, 1932, with cachet (lot 21); a set of three covers initialed and addressed by the president commemorating the fourth presidential cruise of 1939 and bearing three *USS Houston* postmarks: February 18, Departure Key West, Florida; February 27, Fleet Problem Twenty; and March 3, Arrival Charleston (lot 23); and an August 12, 1918, "Inauguration of first aerial mail line" cover postmarked "Air Mail Service Washington Aug. 11, 12 P.M. 1918" (lot 24). These lots sold for $327.

Twenty-seven lots (28-54), consisting of bundles of from eight to 200 National Airmail Week covers, all addressed to the president and all, except the last three lots, bearing cachets, were placed on the block. Most covers bore signatures of postmasters around the country, and many also included signatures of the pilots who flew the covers. Literally thousands of different cachets and postmarks were represented by these covers. They sold for $1,121.

The next 24 lots (55-78) featured another section of National Airmail Week covers, all first-flight covers, many bearing the signatures of the pilots making the flights. These lots were sold in bundles of from eight to 50 covers and sold for $493.

Covers bearing interesting autographs and addressed to the president were next on the agenda. These 12 lots (79-90) featured a 1935 Mitchell Trophy Race cover signed by Eddie Rickenbacker, Gar Wood and James Doolittle (lot 79); a National Airmail Week cover postmarked Marquette, Michigan, and signed by Orville Wright (82); and a first-day cover for the U.S. 3¢ Hawaii Territorial issue of 1937 (Scott 799), signed by Hawaiian Princess Theresa Quana Kaohelelani (lot 84). These lots sold for $232.

A selection of 18 lots (91-108) of post office dedication covers, most signed by postmasters, and postmarks were offered. Lot 95 was a cover from the post office dedication in Rhinebeck, New York, sent to the president by his secretary, Marguerite LeHand, along with a note reading:

> "Dear Franklin,
>   I hope you get this safely!
>   I send it just in case 'they' should not think of sending you one from the post-office. It's been such a nice week end.
>   Margaret"

Lot 107 was a cover sent from the Dominican Republic to the United States, receiving postmarks along the way from Great Britain, Belgium, Argentina, Chile and Canada. The cover took one year to reach its destination.

These 18 lots realized $260.50.

Washingtonia made up the next eight lots (109-16) and included first-day covers with different cachets for the 1942 Win the War stamp (Scott 905), the 1943 Nations United for Victory issue (Scott 907) and the 1943 Four Freedoms issue (Scott 908). These lots sold for $269.

Eleven lots (117-27) of covers bearing Naval postmarks sold for $181.50 and were followed by two lots (128-29) of Christmas greeting covers addressed to the president, which sold for $30.

The Texas centennial celebration of 1935 was represented by two lots (130-31) of 20 and 27 covers with various cachets and signed by postmasters and the governor of Texas. These sold for $25 and were followed by a single lot of three pictorially addressed covers (lot 132) that sold for $7, and 15 lots (133-47) of various first-flight covers that sold for $409.

Some of the most interesting items yet seen were offered in 66 lots (148-213) of miscellaneous covers.

Lot 148 was a piece of Alaskan tree bark used as a first-flight postcard for the May 8, 1938, Fairbanks-to-Juneau flight, and bearing a special cachet. Lot 174 was a Pony Express cover from Nacona, Texas, to San Francisco, made entirely of leather with the address sewn in brown thread. Lot 178 was a 1942 prisoner-of-war Christmas greeting from Stalag VIIIb addressed to the president and Mrs. Roosevelt. Lot 187 was an official envelope bearing a set of eight stamps from Nepal in front and several Indian stamps on the reverse and sent to FDR from the August 1939 Denis-Roosevelt Asiatic Expedition. The cover contained a letter to "Dear Cousin Franklin" from "Leila" and read, in part:

> "His Highness, the Maharajah of Nepal asked me to con-
> vey to you his greetings . . .
> "He also owns a hat, which I held in my hands, and which
> is actually and truly worth five million dollars."

Other lots in this section featured first-day covers, war cachets, Antarctic Expedition covers, Anti-Axis cachets, and inaugural and Birthday covers among others. These 66 lots were gaveled down at $730.

"Covers addressed to the President from other countries" made up the next 25 lots (214-38) offered. Items included a 1941 Bahamas sea-floor cover posted at the bottom of the sea in Williamson Photosphere (lot 214); a cover from the Netherlands addressed "To Very Much Grandiose: Excellent Grandiose: His High Dear: High High Right Honourable His Excellency: His Esquire: His Reverence: The President of Government of: United States of America, Roosevelt" (lot 224); and a May 22, 1939, letter sent to FDR from Philippine President Quezon, which was sent by clipper mail to San Francisco and then by Pony Express to Washington (lot 229). Figure 76 shows FDR's copy of a Mulready envelope, used in Great Britain before the issuance of the Penny Black, as well as a satirical envelope known as the Pickwick envelope (Figure 77). These lots were sold for a total of $454.

The final 63 lots of this first session comprised complete mint sheets of U.S. stamps issued during the Roosevelt administration and containing autographs of the president and Treasury Secretary Henry Morgenthau Jr. in the margins (lots 239-301). These lots were originally sold in the first auction and were being reoffered by the original purchaser.

Sheets included, among others, the 1933 Newburgh Peace issue (Scott 727), 1934 Mothers of America (Scott 738), 1936-37 Army-Navy series (Scott 785-94), 1940 Pan American Union (Scott 895) and a sheet of 50 1938 6¢ air-

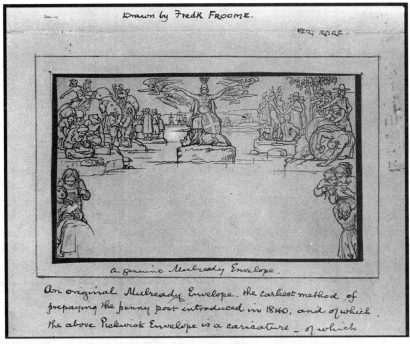

Figure 76. This is the Mulready envelope from the Roosevelt collection.

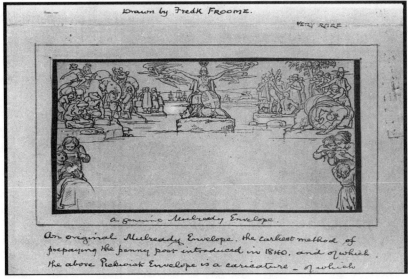

Figure 77. The satirical Pickwick envelope from the Roosevelt collection.

mail stamps (Scott C23).

These final lots sold for $8,414 and brought the total amount for this first session to $13,771.50.

Fourth Sale, Second Session, Wednesday, December 18, 1946, 2 p.m.

The second portion of the fourth sale number 16271, American Sale number 371, opened at 2 p.m. on December 18. Many of the items in this session, as well as the autographed sheets in the first session, were items that had been sold during the first sale in April and were being offered by the owners. In the introduction to the auction catalog, Harmers mentioned these items to bidders:

"Several purchasers in earlier sales have decided to dispose of part of their holdings in this fourth auction. Actually the stamps are largely the property of two buyers, one group mainly comprising autographed sheets and the other part of the Hong Kong collection and other items bought on April 2nd. These properties are clearly classified in this catalogue and the stamps are similarly described as when previously offered."

The first lot (302) was a small die proof of the 2¢ 1909 Hudson-Fulton issue (Scott 372p) along with a normal and imperforate copy of the stamp (Scott 372 & 373), which sold for $150. It was followed by one lot featuring an 1899 $500 revenue stamp (Scott R180) and a lot featuring the 14-centavo, 1-real and 2r values from the 1854 Philippines issues (Scott 4, 16 and 17). These two lots (303, 304) sold for $65.

Three lots (305-7) of Argentine stamps, taken from a collection presented to FDR by Argentine collectors on the president's trip to Buenos Aires in 1936, were followed by two lots (308-9) of Argentina from the president's personal collection. These lots sold for $82.

Offered next were 73 lots (310-82) of foreign stamps and covers, including issues from Austria (lot 310); Barbados, Dominica, Grenada and Jamaica (311); Basutoland (312); Brazil (313); Czechoslovakia (314); Dominican Republic (315-31); Germany (332); Guatemala (333); Haiti (334-35); Hong Kong, taken from the president's specialized collection and mostly mounted on album pages and written up by FDR (336-50); Jamaica (351); Leeward Islands (353); Montserrat (354); Newfoundland (355); New Zealand (356); Papua (357); Persia (358); Peru (359); St. Vincent (360); Spain (361); Straits Settlements (362); Syria (363); Togo (364); Tonga Tin Can Mail (365); Trinidad (366); Trinidad and Tobago (367-68); Turks and Caicos Islands (369); Union of South Africa (370-74); Uruguay (375-82); and Yugoslavia (352). Figure 78 shows a 1912 sheet of stamps from Tibet. These lots sold for a combined total of $1,363.50.

A section of 24 lots (383-406) of miscellaneous items was offered next. Items included a collection of 48 battleship covers from 1861 through 1931 in a loose-leaf scrapbook (lot 383); a large box filled with several thousand stamps sorted into envelopes and bearing the name of each country in the president's hand (388); covers bearing cancels of towns named Franklin, Delano, Roosevelt and others (lots 395-401); and a set of six first-day covers on "Official Business-Postmaster General" envelopes addressed to presidential secretary Marguerite LeHand, each bearing a letter signed by PMG Farley (lot 402). These lots brought in an additional $1,313.

A selection of U.S. and foreign covers not addressed to the president was presented in 26 lots (407-32).

Included was a May 23, 1932, transatlantic solo flight cover bearing New York May 13 and Londonderry May 23 postmarks and a special cachet, signed by Amelia Earhart as cover 49 of 50 carried on the flight (lot 408); a 1929 Zeppelin "Round the World" flown cover (410); two lots of Highway Mail Service covers (413-14); and seven covers commemorating the 1939 visit of King George VI and Queen Elizabeth with Royal Train postmarks (430). These covers sold for $340.

Next followed a selection of five lots of items that did not come from the Roosevelt collection. In the introduction to catalog four, Harmers explained the presence of these five lots:

"We have been requested to include a very rare and unusual sheet of Greece showing a double printing, probably unique, a Cape Cod cover and some other items that come under the classification of Rooseveltiana. As this will be the last occasion when the items could be offered in such excellent company we have agreed to accept them."

The first of these five lots (433) was a complete mint sheet of the 30-drachma Roosevelt memorial stamp from Greece (Scott 469), described as

Figure 78. This 1912 sheet of Tibet stamps was in the FDR collection.

"showing one complete double impression chiefly visible in the portrait and two partial double impressions on the 36th to 38th stamps. This item is probably unique and of extreme interest and rarity." This sheet sold for $150.

Lot 434 included three letters signed by Franklin D. Roosevelt as governor of New York, acknowledging gifts of stamps sent to him. The letters sold for $50.

Lot 435 featured correspondence from the Civil Service commission in the form of three letters signed by Charles Lyman and Theodore Roosevelt. The lot sold for $25.

Lot 436 consisted of autographed photographs of former Presidents Theodore Roosevelt and Calvin Coolidge. These sold for $35.

The final lot (437) offered by private owners and not part of the Roosevelt collection was a July 1931 United States-to-Turkey-by-Cape Cod flown cover bearing an official cachet and addressed to and autographed by the president. The cover includes photographs of the pilots and a map showing the route of their flight. The cover sold for $35.

Another huge selection of American Consular Service correspondence was offered in 73 lots (438-510). All featured stamps on portions of heavy registered mail and contained many blocks and high-value stamps.

American Consular Service correspondence was sent from offices all over the world to Washington, and pieces in these lots were represented by: Abyssinia (lots 438-39), Aden (440), Australia (441), Austria (442-45), Bahamas (446-51), Barbados (452-59), Bermuda (460-64), British Guiana (465), British Honduras (466-68), Burma (469-70), Danzig (471-72), Denmark (473), Dutch Indies (474), French Colonies (475), Gibraltar (476), Hong Kong (477-81), Indo-China (482), Irish Free State (483), Jamaica (484), Kenya and Uganda (485-86), Malta (487), Newfoundland (488-92), New Zealand (493), Philippines (494), Sweden (495), Trinidad and Tobago (496), British Empire (497) and miscellaneous foreign (498-510).

The lots of American Consular correspondence netted an additional $1,302 for the estate.

Twelve lots (511-22) of large boxes containing thousands of covers and stamps were auctioned. The first two lots (511-12) were large 26-inch by 17-inch by 11½-inch boxes containing approximately 4,500 to 5,000 covers from all parts of the world addressed to FDR, including many first flights, airmails and commemoratives. These were followed by 10 lots of boxes containing hundreds of covers and thousands of stamps cut from official correspondence. These 12 lots sold for a total of $3,515.

Eight lots (523-30) of the president's binders were presented next. Included were binders that held FDR's collections of British Empire stamps, Bermuda, Hong Kong, Great Britain, Netherlands, Danish and French West Indies, and U.S. commemorative and airpost collections. The binders sold for a combined total of $204.

Philatelic literature made up the next 11 lots (531-41) offered. Included were the president's Scott *U.S. Specialized* catalog from 1942 and *Standard Postage Stamp* catalog from 1945, both imprinted "Franklin D. Roosevelt" in gold lettering on the front cover (lots 531 and 533); a copy of *The American Air Mail Catalogue* by the American Air Mail Society 1940, specially prepared for the president and signed by the board of editors, section chairman and assistants (lot 534); and a lot (541) of various pamphlets, periodicals, price lists and auction catalogs. The philatelic literature sold for a total of $225.

The final lot of the fourth sale consisted of 17 linen-covered boxes of three sizes with hinged tops and two pocket-size imitation leather-bound stock books. This final lot sold for $27.50.

The second session of the fourth sale accounted for sale totals of $8,865.50. The grand total from the fourth sale auction totaled $22,637.00.

Thus ended the auction of the Franklin D. Roosevelt stamp collection. It had taken four auctions totaling seven days in February, April, July and December of 1946, and untold man-hours to sort and catalog the thousands of items that made up the president's collection.

The result was well over $225,000 for the Roosevelt estate from a collection appraised at roughly $80,000. It brought serious philatelists and weekend stamp collectors together to buy items for their collections, as well as hundreds of people who admired the president and simply wished to have a memento of him via the hobby that he loved.

Feedback on the Auction of the Roosevelt Collection

As the auction of material from the Roosevelt collection progressed during 1946, and collectors and dealers were happily bidding far and above catalog value for the many thousands of items making up the collection, many collectors, dealers and publications made known their anxiety about the auction and their thoughts regarding the overinflated prices being realized by the stamps, covers and especially the die proofs.

In a short two-paragraph story in its February 18, 1946, edition, *Life* magazine covered the first sale held on February 4-5:

> "The stamp collection of the late President Roosevelt . . . provided him with a vast knowledge of geography and history. The President said many times that it provided him with his greatest relaxation. Last week it provided his estate with a six-figure increment . . . 800 eager philatelists bid above-market prices for stamps that had the added value of being the former property of Roosevelt. A group of 967 Costa Rica stamps, valued at $700, sold for $3,250. A block of Brazilian stamps, valued at $500, went for $1,600." The auction "brought in . . . $54,550 more than the appraised value of the entire collection.
>
> "... In it were stamp die proofs which started a small dis-

pute. A few philatelists argued although they had been given to Roosevelt, they really belonged to the government . . . Most interesting item was of doubtful philatelic value, a batch of envelopes with scurrilous nicknames for the President . . ."[14]

In its March 1946 edition, *Hobbies* magazine took umbrage with the coverage of the auction by the philatelic press, the value of the president's collection and the fact that many referred to the Roosevelt collection as the "First" collection in the land:

"The press has wrongly envisioned the comparative value and interest of the . . . Roosevelt collection sale." *Hobbies* stated, "This is neither the 'First' collection in the land, nor is it the collection of the 'First philatelist.' Speaking politically, he was, of course, President, and head of the New Deal group of the Democratic Party. Philatelically, or by comparison . . . the collection and his philatelic knowledge were not only not 'First' but maybe very far down the line of holding values and personal skill.

"The Green collection is still unsold . . . that has returned already more than a million dollars in cash to his estate. Compare with the currently admitted appraisal of the to-be-sold (Roosevelt) material . . . Appraised by Mr. Sloane at $80,000.

"Admitting that the accumulation appraised by Mr. Sloane is of interest to followers of the New Deal's head, it is still not 'First' anything."[15]

Hobbies had stated earlier in its January 1946 edition, concerning the sheets of U.S. stamps removed from the presses at the Bureau of Engraving and Printing by Postmaster General Farley and presented to the president for his collection, that these items "were issued illegally, and the buyers ought to be warned that some day they will be seized."

"Many sheets were given Mr. Roosevelt . . . which were freaked up in some manner. Just the same, they were United States postage, and the Bureau had no more right to give them to the President . . . than they had to you or me. If some employee had been caught snipping those out, he would have gotten several years.

"When such issues are sold for the benefit of the family, there will no doubt some day be a prosecution in the case."[16]

In the December 22, 1945, issue of *Business Week*, the magazine stated that the Roosevelt auction "by major league standards, is not a great collection . . . The stamps of Col. E.H.R. Green, have already brought more than $1 million, with further auctions scheduled. Three sections of the Charles Lathrop collection have produced $276,000, with a fourth sale coming up." The magazine was of the opinion, however, that "sentiment may pay off" in the Roosevelt auction.

Business Week also expressed some doubt on the legal ownership of some of the material in Roosevelt's collection:

> ". . . Choicer philatelic gems for which the professional will be bidding came to him as personal gifts. Their sources make their retention by the estate lawful, even though it may be argued that he acquired them because of his position. Columnists and collectors have attacked the forthcoming sale on the ground that the Roosevelt stamps properly belong to the government. Actually the executors are subject to a nice legal distinction to this point. Any gift to a President from a foreign government or head of state is by law the property of the United States. All such material has been sent to the Hyde Park museum, the executors assert."[17]

The New York Times also attacked the sale of the die proofs in its January 6, 1946, edition, referring to the sale as a "racket" and calling for an official congressional investigation:

> "It is true that the auction will make more stamps available to the public, but those die proofs were given to Mr. Roosevelt as an official of the Government. They belong to the Government and should be part of the archives.
>
> "The auctioning of these die proofs is against the ethics of the philatelic fraternity."[18]

Linn's Stamp News published an editorial following the second auction of materials from the FDR collection in April 1946, titled "Hello Suckers" and which was enthusiastically reprinted in the June 1946 issue of *Hobbies Magazine:*

> "A few years ago one of the hottest nightclub spots in New York City featured a buxom female by the name of Texas Guinan. It was her duty to talk patrons into a jovial mood and keep them happy while they spent their money. Her standard greeting when she appeared was to say, 'Hello Suckers.' It appears that the public liked it . . .
>
> "What a fitting thing it would have been to have had her appear at the recent Roosevelt Stamp Sales in New York. Her greeting as of old would have met the occasion to perfection for what else can one think of the buyers of this material at the prices they paid.
>
> "It was the biggest sucker sale that ever happened in the stamp world and any sane stamp man will lay you ten to one that most of this material will appreciate in value so fast that owners will be able to see the ciphers fall off of the tail end of the price tags.
>
> "Yes, some few items will stand up for some time, but there was so much of this material that brought so many more dollars than it will ever be worth a few years from now that the wise boys are laughing up their sleeves.
>
> "The hue and cry about the sale of the proofs in this collection has even

reached Congress where it has been openly discussed on the floor . . . Certainly Mr. Roosevelt had no more right to those items than you or I. To any stamp man who knows his stamps, it was just the same as handing sheets of new $20.00 bills from the Treasury department safes and we never heard of that being done for anyone. However, had you or I had the opportunity to have had such proofs given us, we would have taken them as F.D.R. did, so that is about all we can say about the matter."[19]

Of course, the question of die proofs was settled before the first auction sale in which they were presented took place. Since die proofs had been given to government officials for years previous to the Roosevelt sale, and since they regularly turned up in auctions for the benefit of the estates that held them, there was no legal reason why the proofs in FDR's collection could not be sold for the benefit of his estate. Nor were either the die proofs or sheets of stamps given to the president by Farley ever confiscated from collectors who had successfully bid for them.

Thirty-seven years after the Roosevelt sales, Herman Herst Jr. reminisced about the auction in the March 28, 1983, edition of *Linn's Stamp News.* Here he told of a debate of the time that did not receive much publicity.

Herst explained that many American auction houses at the time wanted the prestige of auctioning the Roosevelt collection and were upset when the executors of FDR's estate decided to auction the stamp collection through the London-based firm of H.R. Harmer, instead of an American firm.

"At the time," Herst wrote, "the regular commission auction houses charged was 20 percent . . . whereby buyer and seller each pays 10 percent. However, even then, to obtain an extremely valuable collection, auction houses were known to 'shave' their commissions.

"The rumor in the trade at the time was that the estate insisted on the auctioneer's selling it free of commission, with a fair allowance for expenses. No American auction house could touch those terms."

As a consequence, Herst reported, many prominent collectors and dealers refused to attend the auction.

The Herst article also showed clearly the profit-making potential garnered from items purchased at the Roosevelt auction. Attending the auction personally, Herst successfully bid on several lots of FDR's Canal Zone collection consisting of about 20 album pages with perhaps a dozen or so stamps on each page, which was initialed by the president. Herst paid a couple of hundred dollars for the Canal Zone collection and immediately advertised individual pages for sale at $35 each. Herst said that "before the first check came in the mail, all had been sold to Canal Zone specialists by telephone."

Herst also purchased the more than 30 albums that housed the controversial die proofs, which he sold within days to a book and autograph collector in Chicago for $35 per album.

Although Herst purchased several items from the Roosevelt collection, he absolutely refused to bid on what he called the "rubber stamped items."

"Some lots," he wrote, "were absolute junk, but the source that could be at-tributed to them made them valuable . . . A cheap stamp from an FDR album looked no different than a cheap stamp from any other album . . . Many of these cheap single stamps ended with a rubber stamp . . . For months after-ward, these stamps were advertised for $1 each by some dealers. It became a joke! If one ran out of those stamps, so the joke went, it was easy enough to get more to rubber stamp for the eager buyers."[20]

What is interesting about some of these editorials is the recurrent theme that the Roosevelt collection was not a very great collection when compared with those of other outstanding collectors. Certainly no one could argue that the Roosevelt collection could be comparable to the Green or Lathrop collec-tions being offered for auction around that time.

As mentioned many times throughout this book, Roosevelt never re-ferred to himself as a philatelist. He collected stamps for the joy and relax-ation they offered him. Any stamp that caught his eye, whether it be a pristine example or a badly centered, badly perforated one, found a home in his col-lection.

There is still some question regarding the collections presented to the president by foreign leaders and dignitaries. By law these types of gifts to the president of the United States belong to the U.S. Government. But there were several items that were sold during the auction that could have come under question in that regard. A few examples would be the gold-medal exhibition collection of Costa Rican stamps presented to the president in 1940 by the Costa Rican minister (lot 595 in the first sale, sold for $3,250); the 1942-43 collection of die proofs presented to FDR from the postmaster general of Canada (lot 438 in the second sale, sold for $1,700); and the nearly complete collection of the stamps of China issued up to 1941 and presented to the presi-dent by Chiang Kai-shek (lots 116-78 from the second sale, sold for $4,700).

Arguments aside, it must be admitted that Roosevelt's interest in stamps and stamp collecting made a very real contribution in some way to the many thousands of people who collect stamps today.

The Roosevelt Collection
1946 to Present

As the executors of Franklin Roosevelt's estate explained when they offered the president's collection for sale by public auction, it was their wish, as they believed it would have been FDR's, that the stamps be made "available to the many persons desiring to secure some of those stamps for their own collection . . . I am sure he would want to share the very real pleasure he derived from handling his stamps with as many of his fellow collectors as possible."

The auction of the Roosevelt collection by H.R. Harmer was a successful conclusion to that endeavor. Hundreds of people attended the auction in person or bid on lots by mail. Dealers, collectors and noncollectors bid against each other for lots.

If the auction proved anything, it was that the sales were a seller's market. Bidders at the auction virtually ignored catalog prices and had largely placed bids on sentiment. Dealers and investors realized this very quickly and cashed in while the market was still hot.

Many dealers who had purchased large lots of stamps began breaking them down into individual stamps and small sets and selling them to collectors with the notice that the stamps were from the Roosevelt collection. They took advantage of the Harmer offer to authenticate their purchases with the rubber stamp indicating that items were from the Roosevelt collection. They also used the small cards offered by Harmer to successful bidders, which featured a portrait of FDR examining his stamps and a blank space for several stamps to be affixed.

Many dealers also had their own cards made up. To each card would be affixed a common stamp or two from the president's collection. The stamps were worth a few cents at best. These sold for anywhere between $1 for a single stamp to $5 or $10 for a set of stamps. Considering the stamp itself was only worth a few cents and the cost of printing the cards was minimal, the profit on these common stamps was tremendous. But people anxious for a relatively low-cost memento of the president were willing to pay for such items. Figure 79 shows two dealer cards with Cuban stamps.

Covers held a special allure for people wishing to acquire something from the president's collection because the majority of these covers were addressed to the president and were easily authenticated with the Harmer rubber stamp. Many people who were not collectors felt more secure in the au-

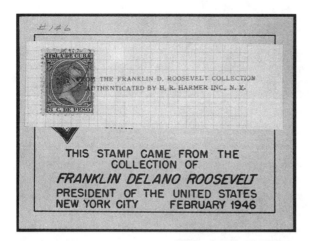

Figure 79. Dealers who purchased a vast array of stamps at the FDR auction created their own cards and attached stamps to them for sale to collectors.

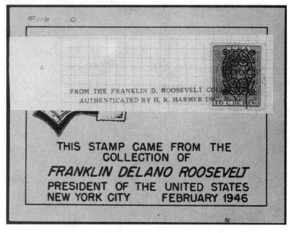

thenticity of an item when it bore the president's name and a rubber stamp.

There was a price to pay for that security, and many people happily paid that price for a cover. A common first-day cover worth only the value of the stamp used on it and the cost of the envelope quickly became a cover worth several dollars.

This is no criticism of the stamp dealers offering this material. It is simply a matter of supply and demand. The dealers made a profit from their auction purchases, and the collectors were able to acquire something from the president's collection.

How much of the Roosevelt collection remained in tact after purchase at the auction is impossible to say. Collections of FDR's stamps often were found in auction catalogs in the late 1940s and 1950s being sold by the album page, especially if those pages contained notations in the president's hand. Cover collections were broken up and sold as individual covers or smaller sets, and

Figure 80. FDR's magnifier, several medals and a few stamps and sheets of stamps are all that remain intact of his stamp collection. These items are housed in the museum of the FDR Library.

Figure 81. The Franklin D. Roosevelt Library and Museum in Hyde Park, New York.

autographed sheets were also regularly offered individually at auctions.

A few items, including the 1934 U.S. Mother's Day sheet autographed by FDR and Secretary of the Treasury Henry Morgenthau Jr., a 1938 souvenir sheet from Guatemala containing a stamp featuring FDR and signed by him (Scott C92), and a few other odds and ends including some of the president's magnifiers, tongs and watermark trays, have found their way back to the Roosevelt Library in Hyde Park, where they reside in a small glass case in the museum. Some of the president's stamp tools and stamps are shown in Figure 80. The FDR Library is shown in Figure 81.

Acquiring Items from the Roosevelt Collection Today

As a collector of Rooseveltania, I am always on the lookout for interesting items. Items from the Roosevelt collection can easily be found today, but collectors will pay a premium for items from FDR's stamp collection.

Auction and mail-bid-sale catalogs often have interesting items from the Roosevelt collection, such as die proofs. Most catalogs include a picture of the item, especially if it is a cover, album page or sheet of stamps. For those that don't, bidders can request a photocopy of the lot for a small fee so they can see the item before making a bid on it.

Many dealers may have an item or two from the collection at their shops and, if not, may be able to get items.

Large stamp shows and bourses are good places to look for material. These shows give the collector the added bonus of being able to see the stock of a variety of different dealers and to do comparison shopping before making a purchase. I made the rounds at a large Chicago show and found one dealer with a small selection of covers from the Roosevelt collection that he was selling for $25 each. After looking them over, I moved on to another dealer who had a box of more than 500 covers from FDR's collection. These were considerably lower in price and offered a much better selection.

Collectors looking for items from the Roosevelt collection should shop around and exercise caution when considering an item.

Use caution when buying small cards with one or two stamps attached that claim to be from the collection. The cards are easily faked. Unscrupulous people have forged these cards, adding a cheap early foreign stamp or two to the cards and selling them at highly inflated prices.

The same holds true for covers. U.S. first-day covers from the 1930s and 1940s exist from which a pencil address has been erased and the cover readdressed Franklin D. Roosevelt-White House. These fake covers have been found with the statement that it was a cover from the President's collection.

Even covers bearing the H.R. Harmer rubber stamps from the third and fourth auction should be scrutinized closely. Similar rubber stamps have been created and applied to items in order to defraud collectors.

I don't mean to imply that there are hundreds of thousands of fraudulent covers and stamps out there, and that each should be looked at as a possible fake. I only suggest that with a little research and common sense, a reasonable and authentic purchase can be made.

Purchase items from a reputable dealer and established auction or mail-bid houses. Ask questions about the items and their sale history. Look closely at each item and make sure there is nothing out of the ordinary about it. Above all, do some research into an item to see what can be determined about its relationship to FDR.

I have a few FDR items in my collection. Some of them are used as illustrations in this book. They make an interesting attractive memento of the stamp collecting president.

Figure 82 shows a 1938 National Airmail Week cover sent to FDR by an admirer in New Jersey. Figure 83 shows a first-flight cover sent to FDR as governor of New York. Both are from my collection.

Figure 82. National Airmail Week cover, one of thousands sent to FDR.

Figure 83. This Charleston, South Carolina, first-flight cover was sent to FDR when he was governor of New York.

CHAPTER 14

Franklin Roosevelt's Contributions to Stamp Collecting

As president of the United States, Franklin D. Roosevelt found himself in the interesting position of being able to advance the cause of stamp collecting in America through the powers of his office. Although many people will disagree with me, I do not feel it was a power he abused. In fact, aside from rate increases and the usual changes in postal laws, the only real philatelic legislation offered to Congress was a bill to repeal the antiquated illustrations law in 1938.

The illustrations law rendered it illegal to reproduce a photograph of any U.S. stamp in its entirety, regardless of the purpose of the reproduction. The Treasury Department had insisted on the law to prevent counterfeiters from creating forged stamps. The Treasury worried that if stamp photographs could be freely used for philatelic publications, publications would be used as fronts to create printing plates and produce counterfeit stamps to defraud the government.

For many years, philatelic writers and publishers tried to get the law repealed or amended so stamps could be depicted in catalogs and on album pages. As it stood, the law allowed only parts of U.S. stamps to be pictured. This made it difficult for catalogs to show varieties.

Figure 84 illustrates a typical page from a Scott catalog showing how U.S. stamps were pictured prior to 1938.

Foreign stamps could be depicted in publications, but the law required that they be defaced first. Most publications etched a line through the lower quarter of foreign stamps.

Petitions by philatelic publishers to have the law repealed or changed were turned down by W.H. Moran, head of the Secret Service division of the Treasury Department. Moran believed criminals would subvert the law and use philatelic publications as a front for their counterfeiting operations.

The law was so stringent that if a magazine ran a photograph or an advertisement picturing an envelope sitting on a table, the stamp on the envelope had to be defaced.

In 1935 *Linn's Stamp News* published a story about a coal and iron company in Philadelphia, Pennsylvania, that used on a publicity notice a photostatic copy of a postcard sent to the stamp newspaper by a miner who requested a copy of one of the company bulletins. The publicity notice reproduced the photocopy of the postcard from "Mike." The photocopy showed

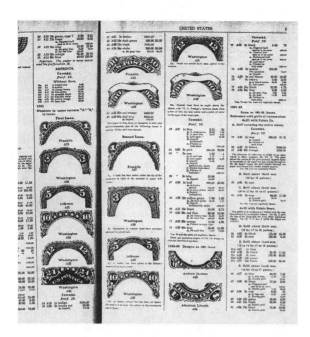

Figure 84. Prior to the passage of the illustrations law in 1938, U.S. stamps could only be shown partially in catalogs, album pages and philatelic publications.

fully the contemporary 1¢ green stamp (most likely the Yosemite stamp from the National Parks series).

"Surely," *Linn's* reported, "we could not even believe that 'Mike' would ever believe that the picture of the stamp was good for postage, yet that is the chief reason that reproduction of stamp illustrations is 'verboten.'

"If you have not yet written your congressman in Washington asking for the passage of the bill for the illustration of postage stamps, do so at once. Washington newspapers state that many such letters are pouring in on Congressmen. Add your letter and help put this over. Congress is stamp minded at present on account of the recent Farley issues and the bill should get attention when it comes up."[1]

But passage of such a bill was not yet to be. Even with the backing of the president, the amending of the illustrations law was still three years off.

In 1938, W.H. Moran was scheduled to retire from the Treasury Department. In anticipation of the impending retirement, philatelic writers and publishers met with FDR and Postmaster General Farley at the White House to discuss ways to convince the Treasury Department that the law should be repealed.

Finally, in 1938, a bill was sent to Congress calling for amending the illustrations law so that U.S. stamps could be reproduced in magazines, albums and catalogs in their entirety as long as they were shown either larger or smaller than the actual stamp. The law stated that stamp reproductions could only be published in black and white. Color reproductions were forbidden. The bill also lifted restrictions on reproducing photographs of foreign stamps.

Congress passed the compromise bill in 1938, and FDR signed the new law in his office at the White House with a contingent of philatelic writers and publishers surrounding him. After doing so, he presented his pen to William M. Stuart, philatelic columnist for *The Washington Post*, who was helpful in getting the law repealed.

Imagine a stamp album without pictures of stamps to assist in the placement of stamps. With the stroke of his pen FDR alleviated one of the most oppressive restrictions to stamp collecting.

This was the only occasion in which FDR resorted to legislative action for the hobby. But he managed in many other ways to make stamp collecting a hobby that appealed to the masses. When FDR took office in 1933, Post Office Department revenue was about $300,000 per year. At the time of the president's death in 1945, revenue had reached a high of $2 million per year.

One of the first things Roosevelt and Farley did was to make commemorative stamps more readily available to collectors. Until this time, collectors had to order most commemorative stamps through the philatelic agency in Washington, D.C. At FDR's suggestion, the Post Office Department opened philatelic windows at various post offices around the country. His feeling was that while collectors would continue to order stamps from the philatelic agency in Washington, most would appreciate the opportunity to look over the stamps they were interested in before purchasing them. Philatelic windows also made it easier for collectors who wanted to buy plate numbers, position pieces or older issues that were still available for sale. Philatelic windows opened across the country to serve the needs of stamp collectors.

Roosevelt and Farley capitalized on public enthusiasm for stamp collecting by establishing a Post Office museum where people could see U.S. stamps and other postal items. This spawned the idea of the Philatelic Truck, a traveling philatelic exhibit of the Post Office Department that enabled people throughout the country to see all the stamps issued by the United States.

On May 6, 1939, Farley announced to the press that the Philatelic Truck would embark on a national tour beginning May 9. President Roosevelt would dedicate the truck in a ceremony at the White House and would receive a special souvenir sheet produced for the event. Farley explained that the truck would then spend several days in Washington before leaving the city on May 15 for its next scheduled stops in Hyattsville, Laurel and finally Baltimore, Maryland, where it would remain until May 17.

The postmaster general further elaborated on the route to be taken by the truck. From Baltimore, the truck was scheduled to proceed "through Belair, Rising Sun, Oxford and Kenneth Square, arriving in Wilmington, Delaware, on the 18th. Leaving Wilmington on the afternoon of May 20th, the truck was to lay over at Chester, Pennsylvania, until the morning of the 23rd when it was to arrive, after a short drive, at Philadelphia. Next trip was to leave Philadelphia the morning of the 26th, spend that day in Camden, leave Camden the morning of the 27th and be in Trenton until the morning of May 29. Arriving at New Brunswick, New Jersey, that day, it was to lay over there during Memorial Day and arrive in New York City May 31. Until June 6 at least, it will be in New York City."[2]

The Philatelic Truck was scheduled to visit schools throughout the nation so children would have the opportunity to learn about the stamps of their country. A stamp expert rode on the truck to explain stamps and stamp production to the children.

The truck was outfitted with specially prepared stamp frames exhibiting all U.S. stamp issues. In addition, showcases displayed various philatelic items, such as gum, ink and paper, as well as master and roller dies. At one end of the truck was a miniature model of a working rotary press, which when operating printed 3-inch by 4½-inch souvenir sheets picturing the White House. "The souvenir engravings of the White House will be distributed free from the truck, and a special junior edition of the Post Office Department's 'Description of United States Postage Stamps' will be sold from the truck at ten cents per copy. This booklet will carry a complete description and photographs of all United States commemorative and historical postage stamps."[3] An example of the souvenir sheet is shown in Figure 85.

The Philatelic Truck was a huge success in every aspect. It brought the stamps to the people of the United States, especially children, and enabled them to see the history of their country through its stamps. It also attracted many new stamp collectors to the hobby.

FDR was also behind new innovations in the Post Office Department that made the purchase of stamps easier for consumers and collectors.

On September 2, 1938, a new automatic stamp-vending machine was unveiled at the temporary post office at 910-912 Chestnut Street in Philadelphia, Pennsylvania. The machine was the product of the Coin Selector Corporation and had been approved for a trial run by the Bureau of Standards.

Linn's Stamp News described the new machine as follows:

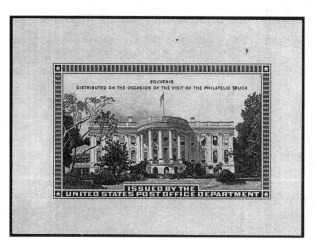

Figure 85. The souvenir sheet produced on board the Philatelic Truck and given to young people.

"The machine is manufactured for mounting behind the post office wall partitions, only a bronze panel being visible. It is the result of several years of work . . . The machines are operated by electricity and can be made to furnish various amounts of stamps. The ones now being tried out by the public vend five one-cent stamps when a nickel is placed in the slot, and five two-cent stamps when a dime is placed in the slot of the 2¢ stamp machine. A specimen strip of 1¢ were sent (to FDR), autographed by Postmaster Gallagher, the strip being neatly separated at the perforations, no cutting marks being visible, nor are there any marks on the backs of the stamps . . .

"When the supply of stamps is sold out, the word 'Closed' appears in a frosted glass window. If the electricity is turned off, the coin slot automatically closes, doing this as well if the heating elements used in damp weather burn out, in this way would-be purchasers being protected from loss of their coin. If a badly worn or counterfeit coin is inserted, these are immediately detected and rejected. The machine is intended to supplement the usual stamp selling methods at post offices at rush hours and also to serve as a supply of stamps to the public after stamp windows are closed. The machines are also made so they will issue a 5¢ stamp if a nickel is inserted; a special delivery stamp for a dime; two 5¢ stamps for a dime; or one 1¢ stamp for a penny."[4]

The new Stamp-Automat, as it was called, was the forerunner of the stamp-vending machines that allowed a purchaser to buy individual stamps as needed instead of a set amount that came in booklets.

On May 17, 1939, the "Mailomat" made its debut at the General Post Office in New York City. The Mailomat was developed by the Pitney-Bowes postage meter company of Stamford, Connecticut, and was billed as a coin letter box. The correct amount of postage was inserted into the box, from 1¢ to 22¢ as selected by a dial on the machine. The letters were then placed inside the machine and a printed meter stamp of the corresponding denomination was applied. The new machine made it possible to buy postage and post letters at the same time from one machine when post office lobbies were crowded.

"The machine," *The New York Times* reported, "which automatically makes one operation of the purchasing of postage and the mailing of letters, simplifies 'stamp shopping.' Within a half-hour of its introduction an eager public had used it for 700 pieces of mail . . .

"Mr. Goldman, (Albert Goldman, Postmaster of New York) after unveiling the device, handed two letters addressed to President Roosevelt to Ramsey S. Black, Third Assistant Postmaster General, who deposited the necessary coins and placed the letters in the new machine . . . 'We look forward,' Goldman said, 'to the time when hotels and every public center throughout the country will have the opportunity of employing the new device.' "[5]

Also mailed that day were 1,000 limited-edition first-day covers addressed to a variety of government and Post Office Department officials, as well as several officials of the Pitney-Bowes company. Figure 86 shows the first-day cover and accompanying insert that were sent to Deputy Third As-

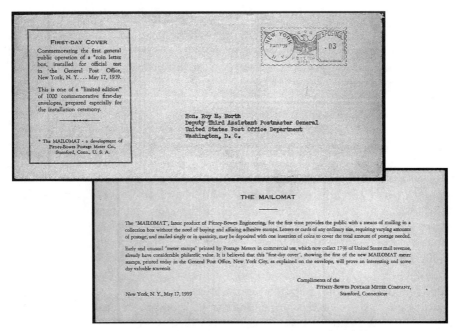

Figure 86. This is Mailomat first-day cover and insert, one of 1,000 first-day covers. This one was sent to Third Assistant Postmaster General Roy M. North.

sistant Postmaster General Roy M. North.

The Mailomat machine accepted up to 60¢ in coins. Letters posted could be as large as 12 inches by 6 inches and three-eighths of an inch thick. Once the money and letter were placed in the machine, the machine stamped and dated it, then deposited it in the bottom of the machine to be removed later by postal employees.

The machine kept track of the money inserted, how much was spent on postage and how much remained. Letters could be posted as fast as they could be placed in the machine.

At the close of the business day on May 17, the Mailomat was opened and 2,156 pieces of mail were sent on their way. Receipts for the day totaled $63.91.[6]

A second Mailomat, number 51002, made its appearance on October 9, 1939, at the Hotel Mayflower in Washington, D.C., where the annual convention of the National Association of Postmasters was being held. It was withdrawn following the convention. On November 28, another machine, number 51003, was installed in the R.H. Macy department store in New York. It was withdrawn after five days due to mechanical trouble and replaced with Mailomat number 51003. Here a slogan cancel was used reading "Mailed in Macy's, It's Smart to Be Thrifty."

On January 11, 1940, two new Mailomat machines were set up at the

Grand Central and Pennsylvania Railroad train stations. The slogan on Mailomat number 51006 read, "Mailed in Pennsylvania Station, Pennsylvania Railroad, Direct Route to the World's Fair." For three months Mailomat number 51004 operated at McCreery's department store in New York. Its slogan read "Mailed at James McCreery — 5th Ave. at 34th St., New York City."

To commemorate the centenary celebration of the first postage stamp in 1940, Mailomat number 51004 was moved to Washington, D.C., and used to cancel more than 11,000 covers during the May 2-6 celebration.

When *Linn's Stamp News* published information regarding the Mailomat in its August 10, 1940, edition, readers were invited to write for information and applications to the Meter Slogan Associates, "a group of enthusiastic collectors," who were making a specialty of collecting meter cancels. Meter slogan collecting had been a part of stamp collecting for some time, but gained new momentum when Mailomats were set up with different slogan cancels at different locations throughout the United States.

The Mailomat was a unique idea for its time. While the basic postage meter was already in use in many business offices in bigger cities throughout the United States, the Mailomat seems to have been the catalyst for the manufacture of postage meters of all types and sizes for all types of businesses, both large and small.

In the area of U.S. stamps themselves, Roosevelt brought many innovations to the hobby. During his 12 years in office, he was personally involved with every stamp issued by the United States. He made countless suggestions for stamps. Nine stamp designs originated from sketches by FDR, including: Little America commemorative, Scott 733; Mother's Day, 737-738; 1938 6¢ airmail, C23; Susan B. Anthony, 784; Virginia Dare commemorative, 796; Statehood commemorative, 858; and the Defense Trio of 1940, 899-901.

In 1934, FDR suggested a new airmail stamp that would not only pay for airmail delivery of a letter, but also pay for the special delivery fee of that letter. He also suggested that a design depicting the Great Seal of the United States be used as the central theme of the stamp. The result was the only airmail special delivery stamps issued by the United States (CE1-2).

To celebrate the sesquicentennial of the Ordinance of 1787 in July 1937, the Post Office Department issued a single stamp to commemorate the event and released it in the cities of New York City and Marietta, Ohio, on July 13. Shipped to the two cities along with the new stamp was a new cancellation die containing between the killer bars the words FIRST DAY OF ISSUE. The new die would forever change the face of first-day cover collecting in America. An FDC of the Ordinance of 1787 stamp is shown in Figure 87.

The 1937 Virginia Dare stamp (Scott 796) was significant in several aspects. It was designed from a sketch by Roosevelt, featured the youngest person commemorated on a U.S. stamp, was the first stamp printed in a baby blue and was the first U.S. stamp that was truly square. Figure 88 shows a Virginia Dare FDC.

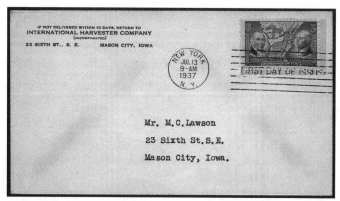

Figure 87. A new cancellation die shipped out with the Ordinance of 1787 stamp forever changed the face of first-day-cover collecting in the United States.

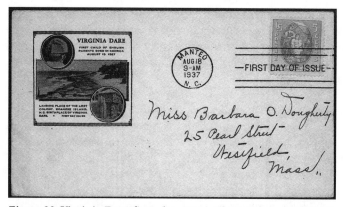

Figure 88. Virginia Dare first-day cover. This stamp was significant because it represented many firsts for the United States.

Figure 89. The Overrun Nations series was the first in which U.S. stamps were produced in multiple colors.

In 1939, FDR arranged for the Panama Canal 25th anniversary stamp (Scott 856) to have its first-day ceremonies August 15, 1939, on the deck of *USS Charleston*, anchored in the Canal Zone. Also in 1939, the United States honored four statehood anniversaries on a single stamp (Scott 858). The stamp had first-day ceremonies in four cities on three different days.

In 1942, to honor Chinese resistance against Japanese aggression in World War II, the United States issued its first stamp with wording in a foreign language (Scott 902). The stamp included Chinese characters reading, "Fight the War and Build the Country." In 1943-44, the Overrun Nations series (Scott 909-21) became the first U.S. stamps to be printed in more than two colors. Figure 89 shows an FDC for the Norway Overrun Nations issue.

Roosevelt was also aware of the impact U.S. stamps could have overseas. Consequently, when a stamp was issued that might have some meaning overseas, he made sure the stamp carried the necessary 5¢ foreign rate. The Kosciusko commemorative of 1933 (Scott 734), Virginia Dare (796), Chinese Resistance (902), Overrun Nations series (909-21) and United Nations stamp of 1945 (928) are examples. (For more information on U.S. stamps issued during the Roosevelt administration, see the author's *Franklin D. Roosevelt and the Stamps of the United States 1933-1945*. Linn's Stamp News 1993).

One month after the Japanese attack on Pearl Harbor, Roosevelt's friend, Ernest A. Kehr, then stamp editor for the *New York Herald Tribune*, visited Halloran General Hospital in Staten Island, New York, to visit wounded soldiers. Kehr met a multiple amputee and began discussing stamps with him. This discussion led to the formation of a stamp-collecting program at the hospital so that wounded soldiers and sailors would have something to occupy their time during their convalescence. Soon other military hospitals around the nation began stamp programs for their patients.

When Kehr talked about the military stamp-collecting programs with FDR, the president was enthusiastic, realizing how therapeutic his stamps had been to him when he was bed-ridden. Kehr organized a national campaign called Stamps For The Wounded (SFTW). FDR arranged to have the new program endorsed by the American Red Cross. The Red Cross would administrate and conduct "philatelic therapy" in military hospitals throughout the nation.

Staffed solely by volunteers, SFTW did not solicit cash contributions, but asked for donations of stamps, albums and philatelic supplies.

Americans responded admirably to the call, clipping stamps from their mail and sending them to Kehr at the *Herald Tribune*, where the newspaper provided free office space and mail-room service to the organization. Many famous people donated stamps and visited the wounded in hospitals to encourage them to collect stamps. Among them were novelist Faith Baldwin, Mrs. Theodore Roosevelt, Pope Pius XII and actors Adolphe Menjou and Slim Pickens.

FDR instructed the White House mail room to clip stamps from mail arriving at the White House. These stamps were shipped to SFTW each week, and each week FDR received a memo from Mrs. Padgett in the mail room confirming that the box of stamps had been sent out.

SFTW also received the endorsement of many philatelic organizations including the Society of Philatelic Americans and the American Philatelic Society. When the American Red Cross relinquished its hospital activities, the Veterans Administration embraced the organization.

Today SFTW is a service of the Lions International Stamp Club, which continues to supply stamps, supplies and advice to wounded service people in more than 130 Veterans Hospitals across the nation.

Collectors can contribute to this cause by sending stamps to SFTW. The procedure is simple. Just cut stamps from envelopes leaving about a quarter of an inch of the envelope attached to the stamps. Pack them securely and mail them to:

> John M. Hotchner
> Vice president
> SFTW
> P.O. Box 1125
> Falls Church, Virginia 22041

These are but a few of the things that Franklin Roosevelt contributed or had a hand in contributing to the hobby.

CHAPTER 15

FDR on Stamps

When Franklin D. Roosevelt died April 12, 1945, much of the world was shocked and saddened by his passing. He was known throughout the world, not just as the leader of the United States during the Great Depression and World War II, but also as a stamp collector who cherished his hobby.

Since FDR's penchant for stamps was known throughout the world, many nations honored him with stamps.

Among the first to issue mourning stamps honoring FDR was Greece. A set of three stamps (Scott 469-71) in 30-drachma, 60dr and 200dr denominations, each featuring a portrait of Roosevelt within a black mourning frame, was released December 21, 1945. The set is shown in Figure 90.

Other nations soon followed. Haiti released 20-centime and 60c memorial airmail stamps on February 5, 1946 (Scott C33-34). Argentina issued a single 5-centavo stamp for the first anniversary of FDR's death on April 12, 1946. The Haitian and Argentine stamps feature portraits of FDR on black mourning backgrounds.

Honduras issued a single 8-centavo FDR memorial airmail stamp in October 1946 (Scott C158), and Cuba issued a red 2-centavo FDR memorial stamp on April 12, 1947 (Scott 406). Again these stamps featured portraits of the president as their central theme.

On June 15, 1946, Nicaragua released a set of six regular and five airmail stamps to honor FDR (Scott 695-700 and C272-76).

Instead of the usual portraits and mourning colors, however, these stamps featured depictions of the president in action, at the Atlantic Conference with Winston Churchill, the Casablanca Conference with French Generals de Gaulle and Giraud, the Teheran Conference with Joseph Stalin and signing the declaration of war against Japan in 1941, as well as a sculpted bust of FDR.

The 4c stamp (Scott 695) was decidedly different, for this stamp was the

Figure 90. The first stamps commemorating FDR after his death were this set of three from Greece.

133

Figure 91. Nicaragua portrays FDR as a "Filatelisto," stamp collector.

first to depict FDR the stamp collector. This green-and-black "Roosevelt Filatelista" issue, shown in Figure 91, portrays FDR sitting at his desk, surrounded by stamp albums and examining a stamp through a magnifying glass.

On May 15, 1947, the principality of Monaco issued a single 50-centime violet airmail stamp to commemorate its participation in the Centenary International Philatelic Exhibition (CIPEX) held in New York City that month. This stamp (Scott C16) shows Roosevelt relaxing with his stamps and surrounded by his many stamp albums.

The stamp has a design error. Roosevelt has been given six fingers on his right hand, which is holding the stamp. When the error was discovered, many believed Monaco would recall the stamp and make the necessary changes to the design. Monaco did not recall the stamp. It can be obtained today for less than 50¢.

To portray the president of the United States as a stamp collector seemed a perfect way to honor Franklin Roosevelt, and as the years passed after his death, more stamps issued to honor him included depictions of him working with his stamps.

To commemorate the 25th anniversary of the Philippine Philatelic Association in 1950, the Philippines issued a set of three stamps and a small airmail souvenir sheet showing FDR examining a stamp and surrounded by his albums (Scott 542-44 and C70). The souvenir sheet is shown in Figure 92.

Monaco again honored FDR with a stamp promoting its participation in the Fifth International Philatelic Exhibition (FIPEX), held in New York City April 28-May 6, 1956. The 2-franc stamp (Scott 355) does not portray FDR the stamp collector. It features a simple portrait of the president.

Figure 92. This Philippines airmail souvenir sheet shows FDR with his stamp collection.

To mark the 25th anniversary of FDR's death in 1970, Upper Volta issued a set of two Roosevelt airmail commemoratives (Scott C78-79). The 200-franc stamps reproduce the same picture of FDR looking over his stamps, but omit his stamp albums.

Also commemorating the 25th anniversary in 1970 was Nicaragua, which issued a set of eight airmail stamps (Scott C729-36). Six of the stamps show two different portraits of Roosevelt, while two (C730 and C735) again use the picture of FDR looking over his stamp album. The surrounding albums are cropped but are still discernible on these stamps. Scott C735 is shown in Figure 93.

Rwanda marked the 25th anniversary with a set of seven stamps depicting FDR and orchids. The 20-centime and 2-franc stamps show FDR poring over a stamp album (Scott 381-388). The 20-franc stamp is shown in Figure 94.

For the centenary of FDR's birth in 1982, many nations issued sets of stamps honoring the 32nd U.S. president. Again, many featured at least one stamp showing FDR and his beloved stamps.

On April 29, 1981, Western Samoa issued a set of six stamps honoring FDR and the International Year of Disabled Persons (Scott 547-52). The 38-sene stamp (Scott 551), titled "Franklin D. Roosevelt The Philatelist," shows FDR seated at his desk with a decided grin on his face and tongs and stamp in hand, surrounded by a virtual library of stamp albums.

Cook Islands celebrated FDR's birth centenary along with the 250th anniversary of the birth of George Washington and the bicentennial of the Articles of Peace (Scott C20-22). The 60¢ FDR stamp shows the president closely examining a stamp through his magnifying glass. All three stamps from this set were featured as a souvenir sheet as well (Scott C22a). The souvenir sheet is shown in Figure 95.

Figure 93. Nicaragua honored FDR on the 25th anniversary of his death.

Figure 94. Rwanda shows FDR the stamp collector on a set of 1970 anniversary stamps.

Figure 95. This souvenir sheet from the Cook Islands shows FDR as a stamp collector, along with Benjamin Franklin and George Washington.

Turks and Caicos Islands also jointly celebrated the 100th anniversary of FDR's birth and the 250th anniversary of Washington's birth with a set of four stamps and a souvenir sheet (Scott 522-26). The 80¢ Roosevelt stamp (Scott 525) again shows him examining a stamp through the magnifying glass. In front of him are two open albums with four more at his right arm. The $2 souvenir sheet (Scott 526) cleverly combines the two anniversaries by depicting Roosevelt looking at a magnified Washington stamp from his album.

India released a single FDR commemorative on January 30, 1983 (Scott 1008). It used the familiar portrait of FDR surrounded by his many stamp albums and looking intently at a stamp.

Stamp shows frequently featured Franklin Roosevelt as their central theme. The Westchester Stamp and Coin Show (Wespnex) in 1966 produced a cachet for souvenir covers sold at the show. The cachet reproduced the photograph of President Roosevelt seated at his desk and looking at a stamp through the magnifying glass. Below the photo is a facsimile FDR signature and a quote from FDR: "Stamp collecting . . . makes one a better citizen." An example of this cover is shown in Figure 96.

To help publicize the American Philatelic Exhibition (Ameripex) in 1986, the U.S. Postal Service released on January 23 of that year a booklet pane of four different stamps celebrating stamp collecting (Scott 2198-201). The Postal Service also made available a postcard featuring FDR. The front of the card shows Roosevelt at his desk examining stamps in an album, and the back mentions in part that ". . . President Franklin D. Roosevelt was the nation's most famous stamp collector during his years in office . . ."

Collectors used the card to obtain first-day cancels for the Stamp Collecting issue. Figure 97 shows an example of such use.

The Kalamazoo, Michigan, Stamp Club commemorated the 50th anni-

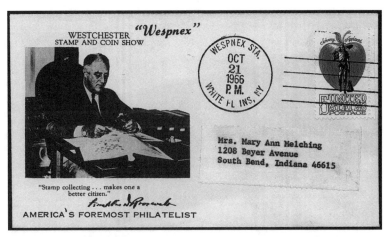

Figure 96. "America's Foremost Philatelist" was the theme of the 1966 Wespnex stamp show in White Plains, New York.

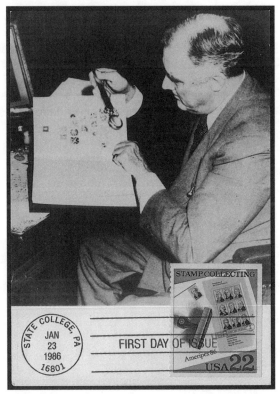

Figure 97. A photo of FDR with his stamps was used as a first-day card for one of the 1986 Stamp Collectiong issues released to salute Ameripex.

Figure 98. Franklin Roosevelt was honored as a stamp collector on the 50th anniversary of his death in 1995 with this Kazoopex cover.

versary of the death of Franklin D. Roosevelt at its 1995 Kazoopex festivities by producing two covers with an FDR/Stamp Collecting theme. The first cachet features the well-known photo of FDR at his desk examining a stamp. The second shows the 1966 6¢ Franklin Roosevelt stamp beneath the lens of a magnifying glass. A cover is shown in Figure 98. The club also selected the magnifying glass as part of the postmark and cancellation for the covers.

CHAPTER 16

Conclusion

Franklin D. Roosevelt was a passionate stamp collector. He resisted throwing away a stamp, even if it was in poor condition. Misaligned vignettes, perforation oddities, color and shading varieties all caught FDR's attention and found a place in his stamp albums.

Covers commemorating various events, including post office openings in small towns, and common first-day covers were as important to him as his collections of first-flight covers and rare or historic first-day covers. A common stamp held as much allure for the president as a rare, expensive issue.

We can only wonder how much more inclusive his collections might have been had he had the time to go through the many boxes of stamps and covers he had accumulated through the years.

FDR enjoyed all aspects of stamp collecting. He enjoyed watching other people, especially children, become excited by the hobby. He enjoyed talking about stamps and could hold his own in discussions with renowned philatelists and dealers.

Most of all, he enjoyed working with his stamps, whether between appointments, on a plane or before he retired for the evening. A few short moments with his stamps served to refresh and invigorate him. He not only derived pleasure from his stamps, he also learned from them.

FDR received stamps, covers and presentation collections from many important and famous persons from around the world. Figure 99 shows a large souvenir card sent to him by Francisco Sarabia during his goodwill flight from Mexico City to New York. FDR followed the progress of the flight and noted on the top of the card that Sarabia was killed on the return flight.

Although FDR seldom could visit stamp shops and shows, he purchased stamps from dealers and submitted bids for stamps through auctions. The Buenos Aires stamp (Scott 7a) shown in Figure 100 was in his collection.

Perhaps his greatest joy came from the thousands of collectors throughout the world who sent him stamps and covers. He received many duplicates, but most of them found a place in his collections. Figure 101 shows a Connecticut Tercentenary first-day cover sent to FDR by an admirer.

FDR also received many special-occasion covers. An example of such a cover, commemorating an Anglo-American goodwill flight between London and New York, and a letter from the sender are shown in Figures 102.

As word of Roosevelt's avocation caught the attention of the general public, the number of collectors, dealers and stamp publications increased dramatically.

Figure 99. This large souvenir card was sent to FDR by Francisco Sarabia during his goodwill flight.

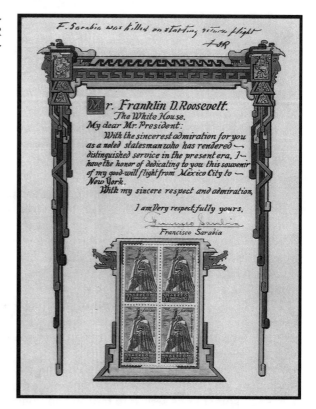

Figure 100. A Buenos Aires stamp (Scott 7a) from FDR's collection.

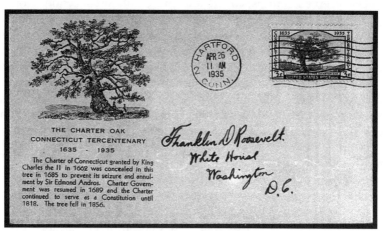

Figure 101. U.S. Connecticut Tercentenary first-day cover sent to FDR.

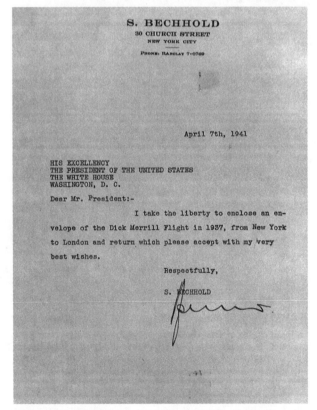

*Figure 102. This Anglo-American Goodwill Flight cover
and letter is from the FDR collection*

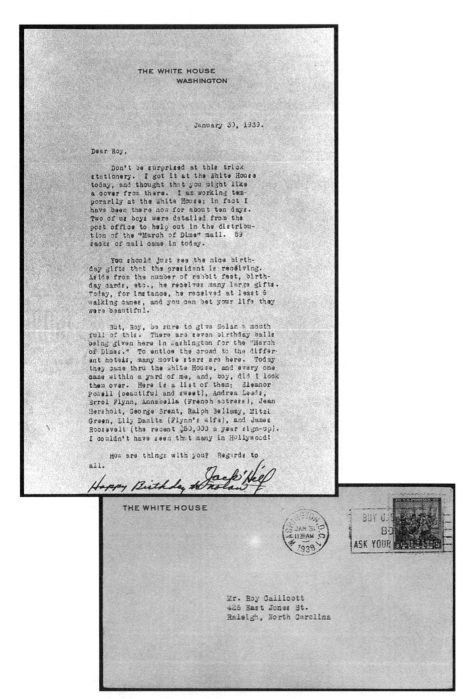

THE WHITE HOUSE
WASHINGTON

January 30, 1939.

Dear Roy,

Don't be surprised at this trick stationery. I got it at the White House today, and thought that you might like a cover from there. I am working temporarily at the White House; in fact I have been there now for about ten days. Two of us boys were detailed from the post office to help out in the distribution of the "March of Dimes" mail. 59 sacks of mail came in today.

You should just see the nice birthday gifts that the president is receiving. Aside from the number of rabbit feet, birthday cards, etc., he receives many large gifts. Today, for instance, he received at least 6 walking canes, and you can bet your life they were beautiful.

But, Roy, be sure to give Nolan a mouth full of this. There are seven birthday balls being given here in Washington for the "March of Dimes." To entice the crowd to the different hotels, many movie stars are here. Today they came thru the White House, and every one came within a yard of me, and, boy, did I look them over. Here is a list of them: Eleanor Powell (beautiful and sweet), Andrea Leeds, Errol Flynn, Annabella (French actress), Jean Hersholt, George Brent, Ralph Bellamy, Mitzi Green, Lily Damita (Flynn's wife), and James Roosevelt (the recent $50,000 a year sign-up). I couldn't have seen that many in Hollywood!

How are things with you? Regards to all.

Jack' Hel

Happy Birthday to Nolan

THE WHITE HOUSE

Mr. Roy Callicott
426 East Jones St.
Raleigh, North Carolina

Figure 103. This letter was sent on White House letterhead in a White House envelope by a postal worker in the White House to a friend as a souvenir.

Figure 104. These two postage-stamp-type labels advertise FDR as a stamp collector.

Figure 103 shows an example of FDR's influence over someone he didn't know. It is a letter written by a post office employee who had a job at the White House for 10 days in early 1939 to help with March of Dimes mail. The man purloined a White House envelope and letterhead and sent a note to a friend for a philatelic souvenir.

Chapter 15 mentioned the numerous stamps issued honoring FDR after his death. Figure 104 shows two labels that pay tribute to FDR.

As with my first book, *Franklin D. Roosevelt and the Stamps of the United States 1933-45*, this book was not written to discuss politics or New Deal philosophy, but rather to look at FDR as a stamp collector and at the hobby that meant so much to him — to see what he collected, why he collected it and where he obtained his stamps.

I hope I have achieved my goal so collectors may have a better understanding of Franklin Roosevelt the collector.

Footnotes

Chapter 1

1. For genealogical history, I used Ken Davis' *FDR The Beckoning of Destiny: 1882-1928*. (G.P. Putnam's Sons. New York. 1972), and *Franklin D. Roosevelt His Life and Times: An Encyclopedic View*. Edited by Otis L. Graham Jr. and Meghan R. Wander. (G.K. Hall, Boston. 1985).

2. Ibid.

Chapter 3

1. Elliott Roosevelt, Editor. *FDR His Personal Letters-Early Years*. (Duell, Sloan and Pearce. New York. 1947). Page 18.

2. Kenneth Davis. *FDR the Beckoning of Destiny: 1882-1928*. (Putnam's, New York. 1972). Pages 76-77.

3. Kenneth Davis. Page 77.

4. Sara Roosevelt. (Mrs. James Roosevelt) *My Boy Franklin*. (Long and Smith. New York. 1933). Page 34.

Chapter 4

1. Elliott Roosevelt, Editor. *FDR His Personal Letters-Volume 2: 1905-1928*. (Duell, Sloan, and Pearce. New York. 1948). August 25, 1907.

2. Ibid. September 5, 1907.

3. Frank Freidel. *Franklin D. Roosevelt: The Apprenticeship*. (Little, Brown and Company, Boston. 1952). Page 87.

4. Kenneth Davis. *Franklin D. Roosevelt: The Beckoning of Destiny*. (Putnam's, New York. 1972). Page 305.

5. Elliott Roosevelt. August 8, 1916.

6. Arthur Schlesinger Jr. *The Crisis of the Old Order*. (Houghton Mifflin Company. 1957). Page 366.

Chapter 5

1. Lela Stiles. *The Man Behind Roosevelt: The Story of Louis McHenry Howe*. (World Pub. Co. Cleveland. 1954). Page 87.

2. Geoffrey C. Ward. *A First Class Temperament: The Emergence of Franklin Roosevelt*. (Harper and Row Co. New York. 1989). Page 672.

Chapter 6

1. Lela Stiles. *The Man Behind Roosevelt: The Story of Louis McHenry Howe."* (World Publishing Co. Cleveland. 1954). Page 111.

2. Rexford G. Tugwell. *The Democratic Roosevelt.* (Doubleday and Co. New York. 1957). Page 38.

3. Herman Herst Jr. *Stories To Collect Stamps By.* (Philatelic Book Publishers Inc. New York. 1968). Page 73.

4. Herman Herst. Page 74.

5. Herman Herst. Page 73.

6. Herman Herst. Page 73.

Chapter 7

1. Brian C. Baur. *Franklin D. Roosevelt and the Stamps of the United States, 1933-1945.* (Linn's Stamp News. 1993). Page 323-324. Also see Chapter 12.

2. Harold L. Ickes. *The Secret Diary of Harold L. Ickes. The First Thousand Days.* (Simon & Schuster. 1954). Page 16.

3. For more on FDR and the postage stamps of the United States during his administration, see Brian C. Baur's book *Franklin D. Roosevelt and the Stamps of the United States, 1933-1945.* (Linn's Stamp News. 1993).

4. *Linn's Stamp News.* May 6, 1933. Page 449.

5. *Linn's Stamp News.* June 24, 1933. Page 563.

6. *Linn's Stamp News.* December 2, 1933. Page 79.

Chapter 8

1. *Linn's Stamp News.* "The President's Stamp Collection." December 23, 1933. Page 123-124. Reprinted article by James Waldo Fawcett from Washington, D.C. *Evening Star.*

2. Frank Freidel. *Launching the New Deal* (Little, Brown and Co. Boston. 1973). Page 287.

3. Harold L. Ickes. *The Secret Diary of Harold L. Ickes. Volume 1. The First Thousand Days.* (Simon and Schuster, New York. 1953). Page 16.

4. *Linn's Stamp News.* January 13, 1934. Page 175.

5. List compiled by Franklin D. Roosevelt Library at Hyde Park, New York, on October 18, 1945.

6. Official File 13. Stamp Collecting. Franklin D. Roosevelt Library. Hyde Park, New York.

7. Herman Herst Jr. *Stories to Collect Stamps By.* (Philatelic Book Publishers. New York. 1968). Page 74-76.

8. Brian C. Baur. *Franklin D. Roosevelt and the Stamps of the United States, 1933-1945.* (Linn's Stamp News. 1993). Specific information on all United States stamps issued during Roosevelt administration.

9. Ernest A. Kehr. *The Romance of Stamp Collecting: Notes from the World of Stamps, Stamp Collecting and Stamp Collectors.* (Thomas Y. Crowell, Co. New York. 1956 revised edition). Page 266.

10. Ernest A. Kehr. Page 259.

11. James A. Farley. *Behind the Ballots.* (Harcourt, Brace and Co. New York. 1938). Page 258.

Chapter 9

1. *Linn's Stamp News.* August 4, 1934. Page 675.

2. *The New Yorker.* "The Great Philatelist," March 30, 1946.

3. Ernest A. Kehr. *The Romance of Stamp Collecting: Notes from the World of Stamps, Stamp Collecting and Stamp Collectors.* (Thomas Y. Crowell Co. New York. 1956 revised edition). Page 264.

4. Lena Shawen. *A President's Hobby.* (H.L. Lindquist. New York. 1949). Page 22.

5. Memo from FDR to PMG Frank Walker. April 26, 1944. FDR Library. Official File 19. P.O. Department, 1944-1945.

6. Memo from PMG Frank Walker to FDR. May 4, 1944. FDR Library. Official File 19. P.O. Department, 1944-1945.

7. Eric Larrabee. *Commander in Chief: Franklin Delano Roosevelt, His Lieutenants and Their War.* (Harper and Row. New York. 1987). Page 24.

8. Ernest A. Kehr. *Romance of Stamp Collecting.* Page 259.

9. *Scott Stamp Monthly.* "Inspiration through stamps." By Brian C. Baur. February, 1991. Page 10-11.

10. *St. Louis Post Dispatch.* June 6, 1943 column by Richard L. Stokes. Reprinted in *Linn's Stamp News,* June 24, 1943. Page 1.

Chapter 10

1. Letter from Grace Tully. March 23, 1944. FDR Library. Official File 13. Box 1. Stamp Collecting 1939-1945.

2. Memo from FDR to Marvin McIntyre. February 6, 1935. FDR Library. Official File 13. Stamp Collecting 1935.

3. Letter from M.A. LeHand. February 27, 1935. FDR Library. Official File 13. Stamp Collecting 1935.

4. Herman Herst Jr. *Stories to Collect Stamps By.* (Philatelic Book Publishers. New York. 1968). Page 78-79.

5. Letter from Missy LeHand. May 24, 1938. Author's Collection.

6. FDR Library. Official File 13. Stamp Collecting 1933-34.

7. Ernest Kehr. *The Romance of Stamp Collecting*. (Thomas Y. Crowell. New York. 1956 revised edition). Page 267.

8. Memo to President from Mrs. Padgett of mailroom. FDR Library. Official File 13. Stamp Collecting. 1939-1945.

9. Letter from FDR to American Philatelic Society. FDR Library Official File 13. Stamp Collecting. 1935.

10. Herman Herst Jr. *Stories to Collect Stamps By*. (Philatelic Book Publishers. New York. 1968). Page 77.

11. *Linn's Stamp News*. "President Roosevelt Endorses National Stamp Week." November 20, 1937. Page 36.

12. *Linn's Stamp News*. "President Roosevelt Gives Page as Trophy for Exhibition." April 16, 1938. Page 389.

13. James A. Farley. *"Behind the Ballots."* (Harcourt, Brace and Co. New York. 1938). Page 339.

14. *Linn's Stamp News*. December 15, 1934. Page 137.

15. *Linn's Stamp News*. August 24, 1935. Page 825.

16. *Linn's Stamp News*. December 7, 1925. Page 135.

17. *Linn's Stamp News*. June 1, 1940. Page 492.

Chapter 11

1. James Roosevelt and Sidney Shalett. *Affectionately F.D.R. A Son's Story of a Lonely Man*. (Harcourt, Brace. New York. 1959). Pages 313-314.

2. Vice Admiral Ross T. McIntire and George Creel. *White House Physician*. (G.P. Putnam's Sons. New York. 1946). Page 78-79.

3. Stefan Lorant. *FDR A Pictorial Biography*. (Simon & Schuster. New York. 1950). Page 90.

4. Ernest A. Kehr. *The Romance of Stamp Collecting: Notes from the World of Stamps, Stamp Collecting and Stamp Collectors*. (Thomas Y. Crowell. New York. 1956 revised edition). Page 261.

5. *Linn's Stamp News*. December 23, 1933. Page 124.

6. Ernest A. Kehr. Page 261.

7. Clark Kinnaird Editor. *The Real FDR*. (Citadel Press. New York. 1945). Page 12.

8. Grace Tully. *FDR My Boss*. (Scribners. 1949). Pages 7-8.

9. *The New Yorker*. "A Reporter at Large: The Great Philatelist." March 30, 1946.

10. Grace Tully. Pages 7-8.

11. Elizabeth Shoumatoff. *FDR's Unfinished Portrait.* (University of Pittsburgh Press. 1990). Pages 116-117.

12. *The New Yorker.* "A Reporter at Large: The Great Philatelist." March 30, 1946.

Chapter 12

All information on the Roosevelt auction not specified below is taken from Harmer's auction catalogs.

1. Letter to H.R. Harmer from executors of FDR estate. December 7, 1945. The Postage Stamp Collection of Franklin D. Roosevelt auction catalog number 1.

2. Letter to The Postage Stamp Collection of Franklin D. Roosevelt auction catalog number 1 by Basil O'Connor.

3. Eleanor Roosevelt forward to The Postage Stamp Collection of Franklin D. Roosevelt auction catalog number 1.

4. The Postage Stamp Collection of Franklin D. Roosevelt auction catalog number 1. Page 10.

5. James A. Farley. *Behind the Ballots.* (Harcourt Brace. New York. 1938). Page 262.

6. *New York Times.* "Stamp Racket Laid to Roosevelt Estate." January 6, 1946.

7. Ibid.

8. *Hobbies Magazine.* January 1946.

9. *New York Times.* "Roosevelt Stamp Protest Grows, But Similar Sales in Past are Cited." January 16, 1946.

10. *Hobbies Magazine.* Reprint of editorial from *Linn's Stamp News.* "Roosevelt Collection." March 26, 1946.

11. Brian C. Baur. *Franklin D. Roosevelt and the Stamps of the United States 1933-1945.* (Linn's Stamp News. Sidney, Ohio. 1993). Pages 167-169.

12. James A. Farley. *Behind the Ballots.* Page 268.

13. *Linn's Stamp News.* June 18, 1938 edition. June 3, 1938 press release of PMG James A. Farley.

14. *Life Magazine.* "Roosevelt's Stamps: Auction Brings Big Prices From Eager Philatelists." February 18, 1946.

15. *Hobbies Magazine.* "Comparison," March 1946.

16. *Hobbies Magazine.* January 1946.

17. *Business Week.* "Philatelic Boom," December 22, 1945.

18. *New York Times.* "Roosevelt Stamp Protest Grows," January 16, 1946.

19. *Hobbies Magazine.* "Hello Sucker." As reprinted from Linn's Stamp News. June 1946.

20. *Linn's Stamp News.* "FDR Collection Contained Some Jewels" By Herman Herst Jr. March 28, 1983.

Chapter 14

1. *Linn's Stamp News.* "Stamp Illustrations." 1935.

2. *Linn's Stamp News.* "Philatelic Truck Starts Tour." May 20, 1939. Page 461.

3. Ibid.

4. *Linn's Stamp News.* "Stamp Automat." September 17, 1938. Page 739.

5. *New York Times.* May 18, 1939. Page 127.

6. *Linn's Stamp News.* "The Mailomat Meters." August 10, 1940.

Bibliography

It has always been a source of surprise to me that there are so few books dealing with Franklin D. Roosevelt and stamps. The following books merely include a few paragraphs or pages about FDR and stamps, but each was invaluable in its own way in providing glimpses into FDR's collecting habits.

Baur, Brian C. *Franklin D. Roosevelt and the Stamps of the United States 1933-1945*. Linn's Stamp News. Sidney, Ohio. 1993. (Book relates stories behind U.S. stamps issued during Roosevelt era).

Davis, Kenneth S. *FDR: The Beckoning of Destiny 1882-1928*. G.P. Putnam's Sons. New York. 1972. (Details on FDR's early years).

Farley, James A. *Behind The Ballots: The Personal History Of a Politician*. Harcourt, Brace and Company. New York. 1938.

Farley, James A. *Jim Farley's Story: The Roosevelt Years*. McGraw-Hill, Inc., New York. 1948. (Both Farley books give first hand accounts of several aspects of FDR's collecting and thoughts on stamps).

Hassett, William D. *Off The Record With FDR 1942-1945*. Rutgers University Press. 1958. (Information on FDR's last days and how stamps figured into them).

Herst, Herman Jr., *Fun and Profit In Stamp Collecting*. Linn's Stamp News. Sidney, Ohio. 1988.

Herst, Herman Jr., *Stories To Collect Stamps By*. Philatelic Book Publishers Inc., New York. 1968. (Both Herst books look at FDR era stamps and relate stories of FDR, how he acquired stamps, his dealings with Max Ohlman and insights into FDR auction materials).

Ickes, Harold L. *The Secret Diaries of Harold L. Ickes*.
Volume 1. The First Thousand Days 1933-1936.
Volume 2. The Inside Struggle 1936-1939.
Volume 3. The Lowering Clouds 1939-1941. Simon and Schuster, New York. 1953-54. (Inside information on stamps FDR looked for as well as gifts of stamps given to the President.

Ilma, Viola. *Funk and Wagnalls Guide to the World of Stamp Collecting*. Thomas Y. Crowell and Company, New York. 1978. (Pages 155-162 give accounts of FDR and his love of stamp collecting).

Kehr, Ernest A. *The Romance of Stamp Collecting. Notes From the World of Stamps, Stamp Collecting and Stamp Collectors*. Thomas Y. Crowell Company. New York. 1956. Revised edition. (Chapter 17 details Kehr's association with FDR and Roosevelt's thoughts on philatelic matters).

Linn's Stamp News. Amos Press. Sidney, Ohio. (Issues of Linn's from 1933-1945 give accounts of stamp releases for the period as well as feature articles on FDR and his collecting habits at that time).

Shawen, Lena A. *A President's Hobby*. H.L. Lindquist. N.Y. 1949. (Only book concerned entirely with FDR and stamps).

Sloat, Ralph L. *Farley's Follies*. Bureau Issues Association. 1979 (Detailed book concerning the Farley special printings of 1935).

Tully, Grace. *F.D.R. My Boss*. Scribner's, New York. 1949. (Wonderful book by FDR's secretary that includes many reminiscences concerning Roosevelt and his stamp.

Ward, Geoffrey C. *Before the Trumpet: Young Franklin Roosevelt 1882-1905*. Harper and Row. New York. 1985. (Good source of material on Roosevelt family and FDR's early life).

Watkins, Thomas H. *Righteous Pilgrim: The Life and Times of Harold L. Ickes 1874-1952*. Henry Holt and Company. New York. 1990. (Definitive biography of Interior Secretary Ickes.)

Index